THE GOLDEN YEARS

Celebrating
30 Years of Publishing
in India

Also by Ruskin Bond

These are a Few of My Favourite Things
Koki's Song
How to Be a Writer
How to Live Your Life
The Enchanted Cottage
Build Your English Skills with Ruskin Bond

THE GOLDEN YEARS

THE MANY JOYS OF LIVING A GOOD LONG LIFE

RUSKIN BOND

HarperCollins *Publishers* India

First published in India by HarperCollins *Publishers* 2023
4th Floor, Tower A, Building No. 10, DLF Cyber City,
DLF Phase II, Gurugram, Haryana – 122002
www.harpercollins.co.in

2 4 6 8 10 9 7 5 3 1

Copyright © Ruskin Bond 2023

P-ISBN: 978-93-5699-061-6
E-ISBN: 978-93-5699-050-0

The views and opinions expressed in this book are the author's own.
The facts are as reported by him and the publishers
are not in any way liable for the same.

Ruskin Bond asserts the moral right
to be identified as the author of this work.

All rights reserved. No part of this publication may be reproduced,
stored in a retrieval system, or transmitted, in any form or by any
means, electronic, mechanical, photocopying, recording or otherwise,
without the prior permission of the publishers.

Typeset in 12/16 Bembo Std at
Manipal Technologies Limited, Manipal

Printed and bound at
Replika Press Pvt. Ltd.

MIX
Paper from
responsible sources
FSC® C016779

This book is produced from independently certified FSC® paper to
ensure responsible forest management.

To all my wonderful family members, who have made it possible for me to write my books

Contents

1. Why Stop? ... 1
2. Mind Over Matter ... 4
3. One Day at a Time ... 6
4. Spoil Yourself! ... 8
5. The Button in the Fish ... 10
6. Our Five Senses ... 12
7. Longevity ... 14
8. Kindness Is All 16
9. Mr Jones ... 19
10. Granny's Way ... 21
11. The Gardener ... 23
12. My First Editor ... 26
13. A Bit of History ... 29
14. Do It Now ... 31
15. One Good Deed 33

16. And Lo, the Onion! 36

17. Granny Takes All 38

18. 7 a.m. 40

19. Early to Rise 42

20. Can't Help Singing 44

21. The Joy of Walking 47

22. Waves of Humanity 50

23. Quiet Places 53

24. The Lonely Times 55

25. An Empty Room 58

26. Solitude 61

27. An Ageless Joy 63

28. Some Enchanted Evening 67

29. Maidenhair 69

30. We Treasure Our Memories 71

31. Everyone Needs a Name 74

32. Twilight 76

33. And So to Bed 79

34. To Sleep or Not to Sleep 82

35. The Afternoon Siesta	84
36. Dreams	87
37. The Longest Day	90
38. The Pleasures of Doing Nothing	93
39. Favourite Trees	96
40. Trees Higher Up	99
41. Little Flowers	102
42. Grow Something!	106
43. The Firefly	108
44. Salute the Crow	110
45. How to Boil an Egg	112
46. That Midnight Snack	115
47. Calm and Unhurried	117
48. Picking a Quarrel	120
49. A Game of Choices	122
50. Laugh It Off!	124
51. The Folly of Self-Love	126
52. Bald and Sexy	128
53. A Goofy Old Man	130

54. Happiness Is History	134
55. War and Peace	136
56. When All the Wars are Done	139
57. Go with the Wind	141
58. Who Knows?	144
59. These Are Our Golden Years	147
60. 'I'm on My Way!'	150

This book is about growing old and liking it. It may be helpful to those entering their sixties, seventies and eighties. It might even be of interest to young people who don't believe that they will ever grow old. They will, if they are lucky. So prepare for what is truly the best time of your life.

—RUSKIN BOND

1
Why Stop?

For writers, the nice thing about growing old is that it gives us more to write about—all those years of love, friendship, adventure, achievements, a changing country, a changing world, changing ways of life, history in the making. There may have been dull moments, but most of the time, something was happening—and things continue to happen today.

Some writers stop writing when they reach their sixties or early seventies. If they have been successful they feel they can rest on their laurels, or that they have nothing new to offer to their readers. If, on the other hand, they feel they have been failures, they are reluctant to impose their writings on an indifferent reading public.

I find it difficult to appreciate this attitude. If you have reached the pinnacle of your writing career, why stop? And if you haven't achieved what you set out to, why give up?

There is a certain joy in writing, in putting words down on paper and creating a story or a poem or a novel or even a memoir; and if no one else enjoys what you have composed, never mind, you have done it for yourself and your own pleasure.

In my humble opinion, the human brain is at its most fertile in our later years, when there's a lifetime of experience at our creative disposal.

I wrote my first novel while I was still in my teens. It was fresh and full of intensity. But then there was a gap—of some ten years or so—in which I found it difficult to achieve the same level of creativity. I had run out of experience and being a subjective writer, I had run out of stories. Then, in my thirties, I recovered from this period of stagnation. Life flowed on, my stories flowed on. And now, in my eighties, I still have stories to tell.

Why do people retire at all? Why does that number '60' fill them with apprehension? Why do they feel it ends the active period of their lives?

It is just the opposite, in fact. We have, hopefully, learnt from all the mistakes of our youth and middle age;

we have acquired maturity, if not great wisdom. We can't change the world. We grew up in a troubled world, and here we are, still in a troubled world. It will always be so because humans are troublesome by nature. But if we have survived into our sixties and beyond, it is because we have learnt to live with trouble.

2

Mind Over Matter

In his old age the great Dr Johnson suffered greatly from gout and other infirmities, but he did not allow these physical ailments to interfere with his vocation and lifestyle. He continued to meet every week with his friends and literary associates, hold forth on every topic under the sun and proceed with the completion of his great dictionary.

As we grow older we are bound to be hampered by health issues—our bodies were not made to last forever—but if life is to be worth living, we must continue with our work, be it for pleasure or profit. It is a question of mind prevailing over matter, and it is the mind that makes us superior to the animals.

Writers don't retire. They don't get pensions or provident funds. If they have been making a living from the written word they must continue to do so, or taxes will eat them up.

Many writers have done so with great aplomb and success. Well into her eighties Agatha Christie was inventing crimes for her detective Hercule Poirot to investigate and solve. P.G. Wodehouse, when ninety, was still regaling us with the exploits of Bertie Wooster and his butler Jeeves, the members of the Drones Club, and Lord Emsworth and his prized pig.

Other more serious writers were also productive in their eighties and nineties: George Bernard Shaw, W. Somerset Maugham, Compton Mackenzie, Edith Sitwell, to name just a few. Our very own R.K. Narayan, Mulk Raj Anand and Khushwant Singh were all writing well into their nineties. Nayantara Sehgal is still doing so at ninety-six. And there have been many fine writers in the Indian languages, sadly neglected because of the dearth of good translators, who worked creatively through their final years.

I have dealt here only with writers but there are so many in other professions—films, music, politics, scientific research, medicine—who do not allow the advance of age to deter them from their creative pursuits or their willingness to work for the betterment of the human race.

The body might falter, but the brain keeps ticking away.

3

One Day at a Time

By the time we reach our seventies and eighties, most of us have achieved what we set out to in this life. Some of us fall by the wayside; that's the cruel side of our existence on this planet. Some are born with disadvantages; we must help them in every way, see that they do not succumb to poverty and to physical and mental illnesses.

If we have prospered, we must be grateful to providence or whatever gods we believe in. We no longer plan for the future, at least not in a big way. But it is necessary that we continue with our life's work. I do not plan to write a fat novel because I may not finish it;

time is rationed. But I will continue to write stories and essays like these, because they can be done one day at a time. And life, from now on, has to be lived one day at a time.

Living one day at a time—or if you prefer, one week or one month at a time—we come to appreciate all that's beautiful and worthwhile on this earth—nature's seasons; sunrise and sunset; night and day; sunshine and rain; the earth's green cover; the wealth of our forests, rivers, oceans. Also human kindness, fortitude, the creative spirit.

There is a lovely poem by Walter de la Mare which I have kept beside me all these years, and which sums up what I have been trying to say. The poem is called 'Fare Well', and this is its last verse:

> *Look thy last on all things lovely,*
> *Every hour. Let no night*
> *Seal thy sense in deathly slumber*
> *Till to delight*
> *Thou have paid thy utmost blessing;*
> *Since that all things thou would praise*
> *Beauty took from those who loved them*
> *In other days.*

Look at everything as though you are seeing it for the last time, and you will appreciate it all the more.

4
Spoil Yourself!

You have lived through your allotted three score years and ten, you are now in your seventies or eighties, you can look back upon your life with some satisfaction, so why not celebrate a little, give yourself a treat? Spoil yourself for a change.

Why wait for another birthday? Now every day is a birthday, every day a bonus. Seize the day and celebrate your survival on Planet Earth.

As we get older we sometimes crave the things we enjoyed when we were young. Our tastebuds experience a revival. We long for an ice cream, one of those large banana splits or tutti-frutti. Or we might visualize those mouthwatering jalebis, all spangled in golden syrup. Or a lemon tart or some guava cheese. Does anyone still make guava cheese? Whatever it is you fancy, send for some, have a feast.

The other day I was in a department store, buying socks. Unexciting. Then I saw a shelf full of confectionery, and standing out among those chocolates and other delicacies, an array of lollipops. Gosh, it must have been seventy-five years since I'd sucked on a lollipop! Why shouldn't I enjoy one again? I bought a large lollipop and, to the consternation of my companions, walked out of the shop sucking it. It tasted better than the lollipops I'd enjoyed as a boy. And now I shall indulge myself with the occasional lollipop.

It's possible that your doctor forbids you from indulging in sweets and certain savouries. Well, you can have just one, now and then. Alternately, you can buy yourself a colourful T-shirt or a silk scarf or a panama hat, but clothes are not as much fun as jalebis, jellies, jam tarts—and lollipops!

Don't wait for your birthday. Make *today* your birthday.

5

The Button in the Fish

When a tiger grows old and starts losing its teeth, it becomes a man-eater.

When a human gets old and starts losing his teeth, he becomes a milk-and-porridge eater.

I haven't got to that stage yet, but the other day, when I took a large bite out of a gorgeous red apple, one of my incisors came out with it. Which led me to compose another pearl of wisdom:

An apple a day may keep the doctor away
But sometimes it brings the dentist into play.

As we get older and our teeth become shakier, we have to avoid some of the things we enjoy eating—hard chocolates, almonds and other nuts, raw carrots, gurpatti (that wonderful stickjaw made from peanuts and unrefined sugar, also known as chikki) … But there are compensations. You can still enjoy plums, grapes, lychees, mangoes; these are my favourites anyway.

And still being an occasional meat-eater, I sometimes go in search of a shepherd's pie—spicy minced mutton with a soft mashed-potato covering—delicious!

There was a time when I used to enjoy fish—fried or grilled or curried—but I have gone off it recently after cutting open a pomfret and finding a small plastic button inside. (In a folk tale, a poor fisherman finds a ruby embedded in the fish he'd caught. I wasn't so lucky.) This led to the composition of another bad verse:

> *When the seas are full of plastic*
> *And the rivers clogged with silt,*
> *The garbage makes a mountain*
> *Of all our human filth.*

I grew up in a world riven by wars and conflict but still free of plastic waste, which only started accumulating in the 1960s. Now we have the wars and the conflict *and* the plastic. That's progress, I suppose.

Last week they found some of our litter on the moon. That's where we will be sending it, before long.

6
Our Five Senses

We have five senses—sight, hearing, smell, taste and touch. Each one is capable of giving us joy.

The eyes are our windows to the world, the great wide beautiful world that is there for all of us to marvel at—the skies, wandering clouds, mountains, forests, rivers, the sea; the moon, the stars, the rising sun—all the wonder of creation. The eyes see it all.

And we hear too. We hear the sounds of nature—the wind, the rain, the sound of birds. We hear the voices of our friends, our loved ones. We hear great music. There is so much to hear and enjoy.

And we smell. The fragrance of roses, of jasmine; of gardens, of wildflowers, the mountain air, the sea breeze. We smell good food—appetizing odours! We eat what smells good.

The sense of taste—we take it for granted, but life wouldn't be much fun without it. If everything tasted the same, from chocolates to fish and chips, we would take no interest in our food and would fade away due to lack of nourishment. Our taste buds keep us going, make life worth living!

And then there's touch. The touch of a loving hand, the feel of things, good things—your clothes, your books, your intimate belongings, your own flesh. Cold and warmth, pain and pleasure are felt by our sensitive systems. The sense of touch is felt in our brains, and it is there that all happiness resides.

Value those five senses of yours. The more you are aware of them, the more you use them, the better you will be able to appreciate your life and all that the world has to offer.

7
Longevity

Longevity. A long life. And presumably a healthy one, or it wouldn't be very long.

The other day, browsing through my morning newspaper, I came across the following item: 'The Harvard Study of Adult Development reached an unexpected conclusion in their eighty-year study. It wasn't healthy eating, cholesterol levels or exercise that was the primary determinant of participants' long-term health and life span. It was their close relationships.'

This was something I had always suspected. Having spent the better part of my eighty-eight years watching the world go by, I couldn't help noticing that the people who were most 'alive', and enjoying life, were those who were deeply involved in close and positive relationships, with loved ones and also with the world at large—friends, colleagues and everyone with whom they came into contact. They *built* relationships, made themselves *wanted*, and as a result they were successful in their professions, vocations and journey through life.

Do careful people live longer than those who take risks? Do health freaks live to be a hundred? Does it have something to do with your parents and grandparents? Does your environment make a difference? All these things come into play, but so does fate, destiny, luck and a bolt of lightning.

As the happy-go-lucky tramp said to the millionaire with ulcers: 'Don't worry. Be happy.'

It doesn't really matter how long you live, as long as you've given something of yourself to those you love. My father died in his forties, but I still feel his helping hand in mine.

8
Kindness Is All ...

Kindness is all.

It's a human quality, but it isn't found in everyone. You won't find it in the school bully, or in the conman who takes you to the cleaners, or in the sadistic killer or terrorist, or even in the intolerant fanatic who wants you to do things his way.

But I remember the kind people, those rare souls who go out of their way to help you when they can so easily look the other way.

One of these was Mr Bromley, head clerk at the Public Health Office in Jersey in the Channel Islands, where I worked for a year. He was a widower whose home was in the north of England, not the most salubrious of regions for an elderly person in poor health. Jersey had a much milder climate, and for that reason he had taken up a job there.

He was a friendly person and after office hours he would sometimes accompany me on my walk through the town; he lived in lodgings not far from my uncle's house. On several occasions he would watch me stop to admire a handsome little typewriter on display in the window of the Bigwoods Store. Till then I had been typing out my stories and my first novel on my uncle's old typewriter, which was in poor condition.

'Do you need that typewriter very badly?' asked Mr Bromley one day.

'I do,' I said. 'But it's twenty pounds, and I've only saved five pounds so far.'

'I'll advance you the rest,' he said, 'and you can pay me back in instalments. Ten shillings a month. How's that?'

So I went home with that pretty, portable typewriter, and I finished typing my first novel on it. I left Jersey a year later and went to London, having squared up my debt with Mr Bromley. But it wasn't just the loan I was grateful for, it was the readiness with which this kind and thoughtful man had made such a generous offer.

The typewriter came back with me to India, and I used it for many more books and stories. After many years it had to be replaced, but it lies in my attic, a reminder of one man's kindness.

Thank you, Mr Bromley.

9
Mr Jones

The people who have influenced me the most in my life haven't been politicians or heads of corporations or saints or philosophers. They have often been humble people who, by example, have taught me to put up with life's uncertainties and vicissitudes and given me a sense of direction.

One of them was Mr Jones, who taught English when I was in junior school. He was not highly qualified and remained a junior teacher all his life. He was a bachelor living in a small room crowded with books, his constant companion being a pigeon, which accompanied him almost everywhere, sometimes even to the classroom. It perched on his shoulder or on his bald head, but its toilet habits were impeccable and never once did we see it embarrass its owner.

When Mr Jones noticed I had a talent for writing and an interest in literature, he encouraged me to read the classics and would lend me volumes from the works of Charles Dickens. I read most of this master's best-known novels, and ended up wanting to be a writer when I grow up, like David Copperfield.

He was helpful to other boys too, teaching the more timid ones to swim. He did not have many friends among the other teachers, but he was almost worshipped by the younger boys. In an age when corporal punishment was common, he refused to cane or flog any miscreant, and for this he lost his chances of promotion.

Mr Jones retired from teaching at about the same time that I finished my schooling, and I did not expect to see him again. Then, after an interval of several years, I met him again, by chance, in Kolkata. He was helping run an old-age home for Anglo-Indians of limited means. He looked as spruce and lively as ever, and not a bit older. Looking after elderly people obviously suited him. And some of his former students would sometimes come to see him. One of them had even brought him a pigeon.

A simple and kind man, who renewed one's faith in humanity.

10
Granny's Way

Some grandparents like to spoil their grandchildren, but my grandmother wasn't like that.

Granny was of the old school, stern and unbending. She did not believe in giving in to wilful or disobedient children. She did not shower them with lollipops, jam tarts and cream buns. If you were troublesome—as I often was as a child—there would be no second helpings at dinner. If I argued, I would be told, 'Little boys should speak only when they are spoken to!'

Meals were adequate but never lavish. She had some kitchen proverbs of her own, such as:

- Small meals make for long lives.
- A small fish is better than an empty dish.
- There is skill in all things, even in making porridge.
- Don't let your tongue cut your throat!

But in spite of her frugality she was not a mean or uncaring person. She saved part of her income, small though it was, and when she passed on she left legacies for all her grandchildren, including me. It does not seem much today—only two thousand rupees—but it was enough to pay my fare to England in 1951, with something left over for clothes, a trunk, a suitcase and even jam tarts!

Her grave is in Ranchi, and on it one of her children had inscribed just one simple line: 'She did her best for everyone.'

That rough exterior covered a loving heart.

11
The Gardener

Granny had a gardener called Dhuki, who was a little older than her. At least he looked older, probably due to all the time he spent outside in the hot sun, digging and weeding and planting and transplanting.

I loved following him around the garden, talking about the different flowers and even helping him with his weeding, digging away with the little khurpi that he used to attack the intruding weeds. And I loved watering the plants, watching the spray from my little watering can refresh the petunias and calendula just as the sun came up.

'Not too much water, baba,' Dhuki would call out. 'Or they will all be drowned!'

Granny seldom spoke about my grandfather, who had passed away when I was still an infant, but Dhuki often spoke of him, about his love for the garden and the orchard behind the house. Grandfather had planted all the trees himself—the lime trees, the grapefruit or 'pomelos' as we called them, the lychees and mangoes, the peaches and pomegranate, and also the big jackfruit tree that gave welcome shade to the kitchen and back veranda. He had also supervised the building of the house—a simple, typical 'railway' bungalow, for Grandfather had retired from the Northern Railways and saw everything in terms of straight lines and square railway restrooms! His big railway armchair still stood on the front veranda.

Dhuki had been the gardener ever since the house was built, and I would see him every winter when I came down from my boarding school in Shimla for the holidays. By the time I returned to school in March, the garden would be in full bloom—the zinnias with their pastel shades vying with the bright colours of the geraniums and phlox, and the sweet peas filling the air with their fragrance. In those days Dehradun, like Bangalore, was a great place for gardens.

Dhuki outlived both my grandparents and spent his last days working for one of my aunts, who had inherited the house. He never failed to recognize me and was always glad to see me because of my interest in the garden, unlike my cousins who ignored him, just taking him for granted.

He must have been about a hundred when I last saw him, as old as the oldest trees. And like them, he had seen the world go by.

12
My First Editor

Diana Athill, the editor-publisher who took on my first novel in 1953, died in January 2019 at the age of 101. In her nineties she was writing book reviews and articles, and driving her Morris Minor car about the streets of London. As far as I know, no one was injured.

My relationship with Diana was both professional and personal. I was an unknown writer who had just turned eighteen when the typescript of *The Room on the Roof* landed on her desk at the firm of André Deutsch Ltd, where she was a junior partner. It had already been rejected by two or three well-known publishers. But

Diana saw something in it—a certain youthful intensity, perhaps—and she wrote to me, saying they might be interested in publishing the novel if I were to do some more work on it. Diana and André Deutsch took me out to lunch. Encouraged by their interest, I set to work on a second draft, writing in the evenings after returning from the office where I worked as a junior clerk.

Diana was at least fifteen years older than me, but we became good friends and she took an interest in my welfare. Sometimes she had me over at her flat in Regent's Park, which she shared with her cousin Barbara, a journalist who would one day edit *The Economist*. Barbara had a boyfriend, Anthony Smith, who had written a travel book called *Blind White Fish in Persia*. I was now moving in literary circles, dining with writers and publishers, all of them much older than me.

The second draft led to a third, and finally, after months of effort, I signed a contract with André Deutsch and received an advance of fifty pounds, which was the standard in 1954. Another year passed and the book still hadn't been published! Forty pounds was the cost of a passage to India on a P&O liner, and I came home wondering if my book would ever see the light of day. I made a living writing for magazines and newspapers. Then, a year after my return to India, a copy of *The Room on the Roof* arrived on my desk. Patience and hard work had been rewarded, and at last I was a real author!

Diana Athill was a good letter-writer, and we corresponded over the years. After some time she began writing her own books, memoirs mostly, and achieved literary success with a book called *Stet*, which recalled her days as an editor and had some entertaining chapters on some of the writers she had published, including V.S. Naipaul.

The publishing firm of André Deutsch closed down eventually, but Diana kept writing well into her nineties. And her letters were always full of delicious gossip.

13
A Bit of History

On 8 September 2022, Elizabeth II, Queen of England, passed away after seventy years on the throne of her country. She was ninety-six. Her mother, the widow of King George VI, lived to be a hundred, savouring her gin-and-tonic to the end.

I am no monarchist, but I have to admire the British Queen's dedication to her royal duties over such a long period of time. Her governments certainly kept her busy, both at home and abroad, having her visit countries that were once part of the Empire. She was their best diplomat. She went through her duties with considerable aplomb and limitless energy. It was obvious that she relished her role as royal ambassador, and she earned the respect of her own subjects, the British people, who are otherwise sceptical about the value of the monarchy and some of its members. That relish—that wholehearted response to her duties—obviously contributed to her good health and longevity.

I was in London, a young man of nineteen earning six pounds per week as a junior clerk, when her coronation took place. Most evenings after work I would sit in my small bed-sitting room working on my novel. It took me a long time to finish that first book! On holidays and weekends I would get up late, then wander about the city looking for colour and incident. Early one morning my roommate Praveen woke me up and said, 'Come on, Ruskin, we have to watch the coronation!'

And so we did. We joined the crowds along the route and watched the parade—the gilded coach going by, the young Queen waving to everyone, the mounted guards in their splendid uniforms, all the pomp and ceremony at which the British were so good.

Yes, it was a long time ago, but I'm glad I was there. It is always good to have seen a bit of history—not the wars and inhumanity, but the peace and humanity that can still survive in a broken world.

14
Do It Now

If I am not for myself,
who will be for me?
And if I am not for others, what am I?
And if not now, when?

I once came across these words, attributed to Hillel, the ancient Hebrew sage, and found them so relevant to my life that I noted them down, and I look them up from time to time to make sure I haven't lost sight of their meaning.

Self-preservation is important. We cannot always depend on others in times of need or trouble. There are not many Bromleys in this world. So take care of yourself; look out for yourself.

But what of others? Family, friends, loved ones ... Do we forget about them, think only of our own welfare? That would turn us into something less than human. For if we are not for others, a time will come when nobody will be for us.

And if not now, when? Don't put off your plans, your creative works, the project of your dreams. If you delay and prevaricate, they will fade away, become castles without foundations.

Build castles in the air, but foundations under them. So that when you are old, you can look back and say, 'I built a castle. And it's still there. And it's full of people I've helped!'

15
One Good Deed ...

'One good deed deserves another' is an old saying that has become something of a cliché. But it's true, as I have found out during my long innings on this planet's playing fields. Kindness begets kindness, and generosity has its own rewards.

During a lonely and sometimes unsettled boyhood, I became something of a film addict, finding an escape in the cinema halls of my home town, Dehradun. There were at least three cinemas showing foreign, that is Hollywood, films mostly, and the most popular of these was the Odeon, a small hall that seated barely two hundred. The Odeon café next door added to its popularity. The cinema manager, Mr Mann, had been there for many years.

The one trouble with the Odeon was that it appeared to possess only two gramophone records, which were played during the intervals at every show. Regulars like me soon tired of listening to constant repetitions of Doris Day singing 'Que sera, sera' and Frank Sinatra crooning his way through 'My foolish heart'.

I had an idea.

At home there was a pile of records passed on to us by an aunt who had migrated to New Zealand and I gathered about twenty of these, recordings by popular singers, and presented them to Mr Mann.

'Sir,' I said, 'here are some records. Please give us a change from "Que sera, sera".'

Mr Mann looked amused. 'Are you selling them?' he asked.

'No, sir. I am giving them to you. We are desperate for something different during the intervals.'

Mr Mann graciously accepted the records. 'You are a thoughtful boy,' he said, and gave me a free pass for the entire year. That meant I could see as many films as I liked, simply by paying the entertainment tax, which was twenty-five paise at the time.

Now the audience had a change of music, and I had pocket money to spare for buying comics and fizzy drinks.

That pass held good for a couple of years until I finished school and was packed off to the UK. When I returned, a few years later, I found that Mr Mann had retired and moved to Bangalore. The new manager did not know me and the pass was no longer valid, but they were still playing my records!

Dear Mr Mann, wherever your spirit may be hovering, thank you for all those films I saw as a boy.

The little Odeon cinema has long since disappeared, but it remains a vibrant memory for many old picturegoers.

16

And Lo, the Onion!

Tramp, tramp, tramp.

A friend and I were walking through the hills above the Nayar River in Garhwal. Our destination was a village where a mutual friend lived. It was about fifty kilometres from Lansdowne.

We'd been walking since early morning and we were thirsty and hungry. Our water bottle was empty. We had assumed there would be food along the way, a tea shop or a dhaba, but there was nothing, just wilderness; a dusty footpath led us higher into the mountains.

Presently we came to a small spring and here we refreshed ourselves. The water was cold and invigorating. But it only made us hungrier.

Then, while we were resting in the shade, along came a man on a mule, and both man and mule drank deeply of the cool spring water. We asked him if he had anything we could eat, and he gladly produced his lunch and set about sharing it with us. Each of us received a thick roti made of a dark flour (mandwa), accompanied by a large onion. This seemed an unusual combination to me; I'd never had it before.

When you are hungry, an onion and roti can be delicious, and so it proved to be. As Granny often said: 'Hunger is the best sauce.'

'Why the onion?' I asked our rescuer. 'Why not a carrot or an apple?'

'Because the onion gives you strength,' he said. 'Carrots are for rabbits and apples for children. Men who walk long distances need onions.'

I noticed that the mule avoided both the roti and the onion, preferring to graze on the hillside.

'And grass is for mules,' I said.

But the muleteer was right. That onion and the black roti sustained us for the rest of our trek. And for many years, whenever I went on a long hike or a trek, I would take some onions along with me.

17
Granny Takes All

It's mango season, and the golden fruit is dangling from the branches of the tree. Presently, a flock of parrots arrives. The parrots descend on the fruit, attacking it greedily. I'd love to join them. But even when I was a boy, mango trees were hard to climb.

However, guava trees were easy. There was a guava orchard next to our house in Dehradun, and I made friends with the caretaker, a retired Gurkha solider, who allowed me to climb the trees and, when the guavas were ripe, to help myself to a few. That orchard has long since disappeared, to be replaced by a tall apartment building. I must look elsewhere for my guavas.

My present abode, although perched on a hilltop, is bereft of trees, the surroundings having been taken up by guest houses for tourists. But there used to be a walnut tree visible from my window and I would often see the monkeys raiding the walnuts, even before they were edible.

One September morning I was surprised to see an old woman perched on a branch, helping herself to the walnuts that remained on the tree, now ready for picking. She must have been in her sixties. But she was quite at home on the tree, and she was dropping the walnuts, one by one, into a basket placed beneath it.

I had to admire her agility on the tree, but I called out, 'Are those *your* walnuts you're helping yourself to?'

'Are they yours?' she replied in her village dialect.

'No,' I said, 'but it must belong to the owner of this property.'

'Well, you go and fetch the owner,' she said, 'and meanwhile I'll save the walnuts for my family. Why should the monkeys have all of them?'

There was no further argument. When she came down from the tree, she walked over to my cottage and left some walnuts on the windowsill.

'These are for you,' she said and picking up her basket, half full of walnuts, she went her way.

To the victor the spoils!

18
7 a.m.

Seven a.m. I look out of my window. The road below is empty. Where are all those early morning walkers?

Ah! Here comes someone. I hear the tap of his walking stick. It's Mr Ohri, the retired bank manager. He seldom misses his early morning walk, even though he has a rheumatic knee. He flourishes his elegant walking stick; it's made of walnut wood.

And here come two gentlemen from Landour bazaar. One owns a grocery shop, the other sells school uniforms. They are middle-aged, overweight, and they are doing their best to do away with their prominent bellies.

A few more early morning walkers pass by. This is the time to be out on the road because in half an hour, the tourists will be arriving in their cars and coaches and on motorcycles, and there will be no room for pedestrians. It's a narrow road, and elderly walkers will have to mount the parapet in order to avoid being knocked down.

I say 'elderly' because all these early morning walkers are in their fifties and sixties, and sometimes even older. Like the milkman who has walked all the way from his village (a two-hour trudge up the hill) to deliver milk to several households in my neighbourhood.

He is, of course, walking out of necessity, because there is no one else to deliver the milk. He has a son in the army; his daughter-in-law has two cows and several children to look after. It's difficult to guess his age. The sun and the wind have created deep furrows in his face.

I don't see any young people taking an early morning walk. The words of an old song run through my head: 'Where are all the young men now?'

They are probably still in bed.

19
Early to Rise

Nowadays it seems to be the fashion with young people to sleep as late as possible, unless they are forced to get up early to go to work. Noon seems to be the acceptable time for getting up and demanding a late breakfast or early lunch.

Sleep is a wonderful gift from the gods and we wouldn't survive without it, but to sleep all morning is to miss out on the best part of the day—the coming of dawn, the break of day, sunrise! If I'm up at 6 a.m., it isn't in order to rush off to work but to stand at my window and watch the sky change, from the initial glimmer of dawn to the bright orange glow across the eastern rim of the sky, the first indication of an impending sunrise. And then the sun comes up, sending a beacon of light and hope across the purple mountains.

My window faces east, so I get the first rays of the rising sun. Those rays spread across my bed, my easy chair, my desk. It's a good time to do some writing. And even if I'm not writing, it's a good time to be alive and listening to the bulbuls gossiping on the windowsill.

We who have lived many years can appreciate the importance of getting up with the sun. We don't take the daybreak for granted. We know it's a new day, and every day means something for us. That early morning sunshine gives us energy, propels us forward.

Young friends, those who sleep late, are missing out on the best hours of their lives. Be up with the birds—and sing!

20
Can't Help Singing

When you are down and out
Lift up your head and shout
'It's going to be a great day!'

These lines from an old song by Nelson Eddy have remained in my memory over the years, and sometimes I sing it to myself—rather tunelessly, I confess.

Sometimes I dream of being an opera singer, with the great Enrico Caruso sitting in the audience, applauding. In reality, I have the most unmusical of voices. If I sing in a car, it breaks down. If I sing at a party, ladies faint and gentlemen make sure I leave early. So I do most of my singing when I am alone, out of the hearing of envious non-singers.

Singing is a great remedy for depression. The sound of my voice might depress others, but it puts me in the right frame of mind to meet the day's challenges. I recommend it to you, dear reader. Exercise those vocal chords, strike an optimistic note and let your voice carry across the road and into your neighbour's garden. If your neighbour objects, sing to him—'*Aaja pyaare, paas hamaare*'—and offer him a head massage. Instead of a head massage he will probably give you a headache, with a thump on the head. But there is every chance that he will join in the singing and become your friend for life.

On a serious note, singing (whether in tune or out of tune) does bring joy, comfort and solace, especially when we get together for prayer and worship. We sing bhajans in temples, we sing hymns in churches, we chant prayers in synagogues and other places of worship.

And of course we sing at birthday parties—'For he's a jolly good fellow' and all that—and on other festive occasions.

We sing out the old year and we sing in the new.

But don't wait for the new year. Sing every day. Sing in your bath, sing for your breakfast, sing at the wheel of your car, sing in the lunch break (but not during office hours), sing on your way home, sing to your husband or wife (provided they are in the mood to listen), sing for your supper, sing over a cocktail, sing everyone to sleep, including yourself.

And wake up fresh and sing again: 'It's going to be a great day!'

21
The Joy of Walking

I am not an enthusiastic supporter of physical exercise—how I hated those early morning PT sessions at my boarding school—but I have been a great walker for the better part of my life, and if I am still on my feet today, it is probably due to the fact that I used them a good deal when I was a boy, a young man, a middle-aged wanderer and an early plodder.

I was never a fast walker, and I would come last in a walking race, because I liked to stop in order to admire the scenery or talk to passers-by and watch fellow members of the human race as they went about their business. But I could cover long distances, and when I lived in large cities such as London or New Delhi, or in small towns and hill stations, I got to know them well because I would walk all over them—busy roads, markets, posh areas, slums, railway stations, bus stops, fairgrounds—and this way I kept reasonably fit, as well as found things to write about.

It all began when I was about ten. I'd lost my father, I was uneasy in my stepfather's home and I was happy to be on my own, wandering around the lanes and bazaars of Dehradun, a very small town seventy-five years ago. I walked across dry riverbeds, explored the gardens, ventured into the surrounding forests and foothills and came to no harm except when I tried riding a bicycle, fell off and fractured my forearm. Walking was safer! And since then I have always trusted my own feet in preference to anything on wheels.

When I was eighteen I found myself in London, living alone. I had an office job, but on weekends I would explore the city, particularly those areas I'd read about in books—Charles Dickens's East End, the wharfs and dockland of W.W. Jacobs's stories, the legendary home of Sherlock Holmes on Baker Street, the squalid area of Lambeth where Somerset Maugham set his first novel … I even looked for P.G. Wodehouse's Drones Club, but that of course did not exist. Sometimes I would walk to work—from Primrose Hill down to Regent's Park and then to a side street off Tottenham Court Road. It would take me just over an hour.

Back in India, making a living in New Delhi, I would often walk from Connaught Place to my home in Rajouri Garden, via the Pusa Institute grounds. This would take me over two hours. I would do it in the cool of the evening, eating boiled eggs all the way. Those roadside egg sellers got to know me quite well.

I was thirty when I came to live in the hills, and then of course I did a lot of walking, wandering down little-used paths, exploring the surrounding hills, forests and streams.

In those days there were just five or six cars in the hill station, and everyone had to do a certain amount of walking—children to their schools, locals to their places of work, visitors to outlying picnic spots. There was an absence of litter and garbage.

Today, thousands of tourists descend on (or rather, ascend to) the town, in cars, coaches or on bikes, and there are traffic jams lasting for hours. It isn't much fun walking on the roads. Even so, a few hardy souls dodge the traffic and make use of their feet. These are usually older people, who have been walking all their lives and who have benefitted, both physically and mentally, from the magic of walking in the great outdoors.

22
Waves of Humanity

We have always had a lot of people in our country, but in recent years they appear to be coming in waves. To an old man who cherishes his individuality and has a reluctance to join the crowd, this is a little disconcerting. Does one lose one's identity when one becomes part of the mass of people? Does individual intelligence coalesce into mass intelligence when we are swept along with the multitude?

Waves of humanity ... I began to notice it when the COVID-19 outbreak resulted in masses of migrant workers marching for hundreds of kilometres to get back to their villages, more or less abandoned by the society for which they had been toiling. But that was misfortune, not choice.

In recent months I have noticed a surge of humanity in various directions—places of religious pilgrimage, hill stations, holiday resorts. They come not singly, but in hordes! Cars are parked all over the hillsides; some travellers even sleep in them when the hotels are jampacked. The pandemic is over now, we are free to move about and we must do it in style. Protests, too, are on the rise. Farmers march, the jobless march, disaffected communities march, politicians and their opponents march. They have always done so, but now the numbers are increasing.

The road below my window was once a quiet footpath. Now, from morn to night, I hear car horns blaring. No one walks any more. I'm wrong—here comes a wedding band, trumpeting a popular film hit. The procession moves on, the cars return, the horns tune up again.

Never mind. The solitary human will survive.

I shut the window, close all the doors and curl up on the sofa with a pile of books. In minutes I am in a tropical paradise; or in a jungle teeming with beautiful birds; or I'm on a camel in the desert; or I'm picking strawberries in the English countryside; or I'm at the South Pole feeding penguins; or at the North Pole, fleeing from a polar bear. I can be anywhere I want. I can consult Sherlock Holmes or Hercule Poirot. I can join Mr Pickwick on the ice, or those three men in their boat. I can join Lord Emsworth in admiration of his prized pig, or have lunch with Bertie Wooster at the Drones Club.

Thank heavens for books. The great escape!

Waves of humanity come and go. May they find their nirvana.

Mine is right here on my bookshelves.

23
Quiet Places

An old library is a quiet place.

Readers, researchers, move silently among the bookshelves, and if they talk, it's usually in whispers.

My school library provided me with an escape from the monotony of routine, the noise of the dormitory or the playing field, unwelcome tasks, extra classes, visits from VIPs, marathon races! Lucky enough to have been made the school librarian, I held the keys to that spacious, book-lined room behind the assembly hall.

I think I was the only boy who was genuinely interested in books. Fellow students were expected to borrow a book once a week; it was usually unread. Most of them read comics (the American superheroes—Superman, Captain Marvel, the Green Lantern, et al.—were around as far back as the 1940s), listened to dance music on the radio, went to the cinema on holidays. There was no television, internet, magic cell phones—none of the things we blame for today's lack of interest in literature. But reading was always a niche pastime. And I was a minority of one.

All the wealth of that library belonged to me: Dickens, Robert Louis Stevenson, the Brontë sisters, Oscar Wilde, John Buchan, Somerset Maugham, J.B. Priestley, P.G. Wodehouse, Jack London, J.M. Barrie, George Bernard Shaw, the Ellery Queen books and a host of others. I read a book a week, and more than seventy years later I am still reading a book a week, sometimes two or three. To be honest I am more a reader than a writer, but I will not read anything that I thrust upon myself; I like to make my own discoveries.

Yes, a library is a quiet place. And there aren't many quiet places left in the world. A lonely hilltop, if you can get away from an intrusive road. A forgotten tomb in the wilderness. A hut in the jungle. A tent in the desert. A school during the holidays when all the children have gone home. A deserted seafront, a lonely beach. A pathway leading nowhere. A ship becalmed in a placid sea.

A battlefield when the battle is over.

24
The Lonely Times

Loneliness is hard to deal with because we have no control over the circumstances that have brought it about.

I discovered what it was to be lonely when, at the age of six, my mother put me in a residential convent school, kissed me goodbye and went away. I felt completely abandoned. There was I, surrounded by over a hundred rough and noisy brats, most of them bigger than me, and no one to turn to, apart from several unsympathetic Irish nuns. (I wasn't Catholic, which made it worse.) I avoided the playing field, stayed silent in class and sat or rather knelt through chapel services in fear and trepidation. The walls were covered with pictures of Jesus being tortured and crucified, and the priest, who said or sang everything in Latin, also swung a small brazier from which burnt frankincense (supposedly) gave out a nauseating odour.

It took me weeks to make a friend, and by that time the school term was almost over. I begged my father to take me out of the school and this he did, for which I was forever grateful.

Loneliness can strike us at any age.

When I arrived in London at the age of eighteen, I did not know a soul. After a week in a students' hostel I found a small bed-sitting room for myself; and then, as I had just enough to live on for a month, I took the first job that came my way—a junior clerk on a minimum wage of five pounds per week. Sometimes I made my own breakfast; sometimes there wasn't time for it, as I had to rush off to catch the Underground train that took me to my place of work in central London. During the lunch break I would treat myself to baked beans on toast. In the evening I would have a cutlet at a small café near my lodgings. Sometimes I would treat myself to a glass of cheap South African sherry. I would then sit down in my cold, comfortless room and work on my novel.

It was the writing that kept me going.

It may be different today, but London was a vast, lonely city in the 1950s, and you did not even get to know your fellow lodgers. On weekends I would go for long walks, exploring different parts of the city—the East End, Soho, Kensington Gardens, Tooting, Brixton—but I did not have any of the adventures that befell the heroes of my favourite Dickens novels, nor could I find the London of Jeeves, Bertie Wooster and the Drones Club. It simply did not exist.

But walking is great therapy for the lonely or the depressed. All my life, whenever I have felt a bit low (and the most cheerful of people will feel a little depressed at times), I have left my room, closed the front door and taken off on foot—into the town or out of it, into the city or into the countryside. It may be just a walk, or I might discover something new, something different—an old tomb or a ruined palace, a busy railway station or a derelict cinema hall, a slum behind a swank hotel, a tree-lined avenue or a congested mohalla where nothing grows... These were my walks in New Delhi, or old New Delhi, or just Delhi—a city that can't help overtaking itself in its frantic bid to keep up with its expanding population and runaway growth. Now I find it hard to walk in Delhi.

But wherever you are, try walking your blues away.

If nothing else, you'll build up a good appetite for your next meal—even if it's only beans on toast.

25

An Empty Room

Everyone needs someone to hold his or her hand—especially when they are small children or when they are old and on their own.

It isn't easy to handle loneliness. Joining a crowd in the marketplace doesn't help; you have to come back to an empty room. As a lonely boy I would go to the pictures and lose myself in the world of Tarzan or the Wild West or the mysterious escapades of Dr Fu Manchu or Sherlock Holmes. However, after the film I would walk home to find my mother and my stepfather away on a shikar trip (hunting animals being fashionable in those days); my infant brothers had an ayah for company and my dinner was in the pantry if I wanted it.

But for me there were books. Thank God for books! There weren't many in the house, but there was a small lending library down the road, and for two rupees a month I could read as many books as I liked. And during my winter holidays I read at the rate of one a day, if they were thrillers, and one a week if they were Dickens or Conrad.

As a boy and as a young man (and even as a sixty-year-old), I was always a great walker. As a lonely young man in London, I got to know the city by walking everywhere—from Primrose Hill to Kew Gardens! And here in the mountains I have walked to remote villages, from the foothills to the tree-line. And I have made friends along the way.

In some ways I was lucky, because I had these escape routes.

The unlucky people who really feel the hurt of loneliness are those who have experienced a happy, busy family life, and then suddenly lose a partner and find there is no one to hold their hand. The children have grown up, gone abroad and started their own families, and find it difficult to come home and find time to spend with Mum or Dad.

I have seen this happen to many old friends. Some of them take to drink—either at home, on their own, or at a bar in a club or hotel where they might find someone to talk to.

If you are living alone, it helps to have a vocation or hobby. Stamp-collecting is out of fashion, but even that's better than hitting the bottle. If you have had an interesting life you can try writing your memoirs. Reading always helps. My neighbour doesn't care for books, but he watches old movies on YouTube. Fair enough. I watch them too, occasionally. Walking might appear to be a lonely activity, but a long walk will always take you somewhere—and you will discover others as well as yourself. Get out of the house. The song of the bulbul is preferable to the squeak of the mouse.

And always a pet—the company of a dog or cat. But animals need looking after; they have to be fed and they have to be disciplined to some extent. One of my friends got tired of a cat because it insisted on doing potty on her favourite sofa. She gave the cat away and kept a dog, but the dog would bark at shadows all night and prevent her from sleeping. Now she prefers to live without pets.

'Solitude is bliss,' she tells me. But solitude and loneliness are very different from each other.

26
Solitude

Loneliness is something that is thrust upon us. Solitude is something we seek.

Poets seek solitude in order to write about crowds of daffodils or tigers burning bright. Tennyson had to be on his own in order to write 'The Charge of the Light Brigade'. The thunder of horses' hooves could only be heard in the silence and solitude of his study.

Writers and artists need periods of solitude. So do scientists, academics, researchers—all those who need clarity and vision in their work. But so do the rest of us, my friends. We need to be by ourselves from time to time, to think, to ponder upon our lives and the direction in which we are going. We need, at times, to get in touch with our innermost thoughts (assuming we are capable of having any), desires and yearnings. Only a moron will do away altogether with moments of solitude, because he is unable to face himself and what he has become.

Of course, too much solitude can lead to loneliness. Long ago, an acquaintance of mine expressed a wish to work in a lighthouse, in order to get away from the presence of too many human beings in his life. After a month of self-enforced solitude he fled from the lighthouse, taking a job in a busy pub in a crowded city. He did not want to see another seagull for the rest of his life.

27
An Ageless Joy

In the long lonely periods of my life I had to resort to two different ways of dealing with my loneliness: one was to go for long walks, without any particular destination in mind; the other, to settle down in a quiet corner and read a book—any book that I could find.

When I was ten I could not afford to buy books. My mother and stepfather did not read much; they preferred to go out on shikar trips to shoot tigers. But there were a few books in the house—displayed rather than read—and during the three months' break from my boarding school I read practically all of them. And a strange mix they were, but a mixture that turned me into a reader of almost everything that was to come my way—classics, comics, newspapers, crime, adventure, natural history, stamp catalogues, encyclopaedias!

That winter I made a list of the books I had read, and I reproduce it from memory:

- *Little Women* by Louisa May Alcott
- *The Virginian* by Owen Wister
- *Love Among the Chickens* by P.G. Wodehouse
- *One, Two, Buckle My Shoe* by Agatha Christie
- *Ghost Stories of an Antiquary* by M.R. James
- *A Tree Grows in Brooklyn* by Betty Smith
- *The Little Karoo* by Pauline Smith
- *A Man Must Fight* by Gene Tunney

Only one of these was a children's book. Even as a boy I was never a great reader of children's books, although I grew up to write a few. *The Virginian* was a precursor to the 'Westerns' of Zane Grey and Max Brand. *A Tree Grows in Brooklyn* was a heart-wrenching account of a girl's efforts growing up in a poor family in depression-hit America. (It made a great movie, directed by Elia Kazan.) *The Little Karoo* was a collection of wonderful stories about the Boer settlers in South Africa. M.R. James was a master of the English ghost story. And *A Man Must Fight* was the autobiography of Gene Tunney, a former heavyweight boxing champion who also happened to be literate.

I was to be a reader for the rest of my life. But it was during the lonely times that I really valued the comfort and support of the written word. When I was seventeen my mother shipped me off to Jersey, in the Channel Islands, where I worked and stayed with relatives for a year. But I was miserable most of the time, homesick for India, longing to return. Fortunately Jersey had a decent public library and I scoured the shelves for books on India or the East. These were some of the books I read (when I wasn't writing my own novel):

- *Collected Poems and Plays* by Rabindranath Tagore
- *The River* by Rumer Godden
- *Youth* by Joseph Conrad
- *Rungli-Rungliot: Thus Far and No Further* by Rumer Godden
- *The Big Heart* by Mulk Raj Anand
- *And Gazelles Leaping* by Sudhin Ghosh
- *Buddhism* by Christmas Humphreys
- *The Tale of Genji* by Lady Murasaki Shikibu (tr. Arthur Waley)

These helped me see through a lonely and difficult year.

Reading is a minority occupation in a world that has so much that is trite to offer. But it's more than an occupation, it's a consolation—a joy not dulled by age; a selfish, serene, lifelong intoxication.

28

Some Enchanted Evening

You fall in love and all the loneliness vanishes!

Ex visu amor (a Latin proverb). Roughly translated (I studied Latin at school) it means 'Loving comes by looking'.

Love at first sight!

Perhaps the most thrilling moment in life, especially if the attraction is mutual.

I expect most of us have experienced it at some time in our lives—that unforgettable moment when we come face to face with a stranger and have some sort of chemistry with that person, something irresistible, some mysterious force that puts a spell on us. I call it romance but the unromantic call it a chemical reaction. I won't argue. Let it happen!

It can happen in a bus, or at an airport, or on the deck of a ship, or at a railway station, or at a party. As the song from the musical *South Pacific* goes—

> *Some enchanted evening*
> *You may see a stranger*
> *Across a crowded room.*

In some of my early stories—my 'romantic' period—it happened at railway stations (Deoli, Shamli, etc.), but they seldom developed into full-blown affairs. In Wodehouse's novels, love at first sight usually occurs on ships (*The Girl on the Boat*, *A Damsel in Distress*, *The Adventures of Sally*, etc.) or on golf courses (*Meet Mr Mulliner*, *The Clicking of Cuthbert* and others). And if you want passionate love, you will find it in Emily Brontë's *Wuthering Heights* and Mary Webb's *Gone to Earth*.

That message of love across a crowded room is a wonderful moment, and we have no idea where it will lead us—a brief encounter or a lifelong partnership, happiness or heartbreak. But the moment itself is worth cherishing and remembering.

Love is the best antidote for loneliness. But it's no use going out in search of it. Elusive as a butterfly, it will elude your grasp. Stay still, and it might just settle on your hand.

29
Maidenhair

I was going through a drawer full of old manuscripts and notebooks when a long-pressed maidenhair fern fell out from between the pages of a notebook. It had lost its colour but was undamaged, and it still looked very pretty lying against the white pages. For me, maidenhair is the prettiest of all the ferns—delicate, almost fragile, but held together by a strong dark stem that resembles a maiden's hair; hence its name.

You will find it near water, usually on the fringes of a small spring where there is not much sun nor too much shade. Sometimes I come across it quite by chance, its tender green fronds brightening up a dry hillside. If I go looking for it, it proves elusive. Life's like that. If you want something very badly, it can be hard to get. Turn aside, forget it and it will come to you when you least expect it.

This particular fern brought back memories—or rather, one particular memory, of a picnic by a mountain stream. Sushila, whom I loved, was sitting beside me on the grassy bank, holding hands. She took her hand from mine for a moment and plucked the frond of maidenhair from the plant that grew there quite profusely, and gave it to me to preserve. That was nearly fifty years ago and I haven't seen Sushila again. You could say the stars were not in our favour. But now, holding the pressed fern in my hand, I can feel her hand again and the sweetness of her touch.

Not all of us keep such mementos from the past. Or, if we do, we forget about them and their whereabouts. Some things get thrown away. But some—like a pressed fern or leaf or flower—hide themselves in an old diary or notebook, and turn up unexpectedly to remind you of a precious moment in time.

30
We Treasure Our Memories

Six or seven—that's the age at which our essential tastes, even our obsessions, begin to be stamped on us by outward impressions. They never leave us, even when we think we have forgotten them. To my dying day I shall have a special fondness for the cosmos flower because I remember walking through a forest of cosmos—or what seemed like a forest to a small boy. White, purple, magenta, those fresh-faced flowers nodded to me as I played on the lawns of the Jamnagar palace grounds and today, more than eighty years later, whenever I see the cosmos in bloom, I go among them, for they are eternal, even if I am not.

And to this day I like the sound of a cock crowing at dawn, because this was one of the first sounds that impinged on my mind when I was a child. A cock crowing. Harbinger of light, of optimism. 'Great day! Great day!' it seems to say.

Little things stay with us, remain with us over the years. The memory of a broom, the small hand-broom, sweeping the steps of the veranda, takes me back to that distant but vivid childhood, and the thin dark woman who swept the bungalow's rooms. I loved watching her at work. It seemed like a game to me, and sometimes I would take the broom from her and sweep so vigorously that the dust rose and settled on the furniture. 'Aunty will be angry,' she'd say and take the broom away from me. But she'd let me borrow it from time to time, when my parents weren't around.

The other day, seeing my steps covered with dead leaves, I picked up the small jharoo, the broom lying on the veranda, and began clearing away the leaves. A local shopkeeper on his way to the market saw me sweeping away and called out: 'Sir, what are you doing? That's not your job. Give the jharoo to the sweeper.' Absorbed in my childhood hobby, all I could say was, 'Yes, Aunty,' while sending up a flurry of dead leaves. He continued on his way, muttering something about the poor old writer having lost his balance at last.

Human beings are blessed with the power to remember. But not all our early impressions are of a pleasant nature. They linger on just the same. Like the frequent quarrels that took place between my parents, usually in my presence. I hated these quarrels and I was helpless to stop them. Eventually they led to my parents' separation. And all my life I have felt profoundly disturbed if I see or hear a husband and wife quarreling bitterly. I look around to see if a child is present. And then I realize I am that child.

Fortunately the most lasting impressions are the simple, harmonious ones. Why do I still prefer homemade butter to factory-made butter? Because, when I was five or six, I would watch my father beating up a bowl of cream and then spreading a generous amount of creamy white butter on my toast. Now Beena knows why I am always demanding creamy white butter with my breakfast.

And you will have similar impressions to carry with you all your days. That first day at school, maybe an agonizing parting from your parents. The face of a loved one gone. A pullover knitted by your granny. A favourite toy. A doll, perhaps. A familiar melody. A book of rhymes, tattered and worn. Someone who gave you a flower, a kiss on the forehead.

To the end of your days you will carry that kiss with you. And may it protect you from all harm.

31
Everyone Needs a Name

One day the Supreme Artist, the great gardener who fashioned this planet into something beautiful, decided to give names to the thousands of different flowers that flourished on our mountains, valleys and plains. But he failed to notice one little flower, a tiny sky-blue blossom growing in a rocky niche. The flower ran after its maker, crying out, 'Don't forget me, Great One, I want a name too!' The good gardener apologized, saying, 'You are very special, little one. And you shall have a name. We'll call you Forget-me-not.'

Everyone, everything we love, should have a name.

My cat is called Mimi. A little girl who writes to me from Pondicherry tells me her cat is called Carrot. I love that name! My Granny had a dog named Crazy. He was called Crazy because he would run round and round the bungalow, chasing an invisible cat!

At school my friends used to call me 'Horse' because I had large protruding teeth. They've gone in now, thank goodness; one of the benefits of growing old.

32
Twilight

Twilight ... that brief interval between sundown and the coming of the night. Just twenty minutes to half an hour of fading daylight, but for some it is a time of great activity.

This is when the birds go home to roost. The mynahs, who have been chattering in the banyan tree, are suddenly silent. The pigeons, all home in their loft, have ceased their cooing. The jungle fowl looks for shelter. A peacock finds a stout tree branch safer than the open ground. Only the owl stays awake, ready to pounce upon an unwary mouse. Dinnertime!

In the forest the animals emerge, for the night belongs to them. A barking deer gives itself away, a leopard watches from a rocky ledge. A fox pursues a rabbit. The porcupines are up and about, raiding a farmer's fields for potatoes. Monkeys huddle together in the oak trees, terrified of the prowling leopard. The village dogs are barking. They will bark all night.

In the town the street lights have come on. The hill station's Mall is all lit up. Tourists throng the street, shopping, eating, talking, walking. Children crowd around the candyfloss seller.

In this writer's home the fire is lit. It's November and the nights are turning cold. Rakesh is watching cricket on the telly. Beena is in the kitchen, making a carrot sponge cake for Siddharth and Gautam, who are in Mumbai. Shrishti, my granddaughter, sits beside me, searching on her cell phone for a book I want to order. She is fond of her Dada.

'I'll find a song for you, Dada,' she says. 'What's your favourite?' I have forgotten the name but I remember some of the words and recite them. She finds it in seconds. A new appliance to find an old song. The coming together of two, three generations.

The music fills the room.

Just a song at twilight
When the light is low,
And the flickering shadows
Come and go ...

Love's old sweet song!
Play it again, Shrishti.

33
And So to Bed

What is the most important place on earth?

Your bed, of course.

You spend at least half your life in it, or upon it. You sleep on it, rest upon it, for most of the night and portions of the day. If you are unwell, it's the place to recover from whatever ails you. It's the most favoured place for making love. Most of us are born on a bed, and—unless we fall off a cliff or lie down in front of a steam roller—make our exits from Planet Earth upon our beds too.

When I was a small boy at boarding school, we were expected to make our own beds. The housemaster would come around checking if they had been made properly. He'd look under the pillow to see if there was any chewing gum sticking to it, and under the mattress to see if any forbidden comics or literature was concealed there. My *Film Fun* comics were confiscated and, when I was older, my copy of Émile Zola's *Nana*. Our beds were well-made because we had to sleep on them.

Today, eighty years on, I am still making my own bed. If someone tries to make it for me, I will take it apart and remake it. What is the secret to my success? A comfortable bed, naturally. And I make sure that the bed suits *my* shape, *my* figure (which has filled out over the years) and my tendency to travel when I'm asleep. For this reason I don't sleep between sheets because I get tangled up in them and as a result I use foul language. This must be avoided at the beginning of the day.

Occasionally I am put up in a starred or starry hotel, and the first thing I do is to remake the bed in my room. What does one do with six pillows piled high and three foam-rubber mattresses all set to bounce you towards the ceiling? The sheets are waiting to entangle me. I have to reduce all this nonsense by half before I can get a good night's sleep.

At one of these establishments I discovered a clever room-boy making little elephants by folding the towels a certain way. He would decorate the beds with them. Elephants usually sleep on four legs, standing up. I am told that the guards outside the Tower of London learn to sleep on two legs, standing up. I have tried doing it, with limited success, in buses and on railway platforms. You could give it a try. But not in front of open windows.

I have sometimes slept in dak bungalows or rest houses in out-of-the-way places, where the beds and bedrooms are usually quite basic. This suits me nicely, because I can make or remake the beds in my own way. But you have to watch out for other occupants, such as bed bugs and performing fleas.

The gecko, or common house lizard, is a familiar resident in many houses and homes across the country. It roams the walls and ceilings in search of tasty morsels, such as moths and other insects. Occasionally its tactile feet lose their grip on the ceiling, and it falls with a plop on your bed or on your person. These lizards are quite harmless but rather cold and squishy to touch and we fling them away in disgust.

I believe there is an old treatise on these lizards and the body parts on which they fall, indicating your fortunes, good or bad. If the lizard falls on your foot, you are going to travel. If on your left hand, you are going to make a fortune. If on your right hand, you will go through a fortune. If it lands on your head, you will find true love; if on your chest, you will be disappointed in love. And so on … More fun than palmistry and less complicated than astrology, but of course you have to be patient and wait for a lizard to fall. To fall or not to fall, that is the question.

34

To Sleep or Not to Sleep

Some of us have difficulty falling asleep at night. I am one of them. We are referred to as 'insomniacs', which sounds rather rude, as though we are 'maniacs' of some sort—related to kleptomaniacs and megalomaniacs!

There is nothing maniacal about wanting to fall asleep but finding it impossible to do so. I have tossed and turned all through the night, counting thousands of sheep and goats and an equal number of mutton chops, but without result. I might be dog tired, dying for a good night's sleep, but the minute I lie down on my bed I am wide awake.

I think we think too much.

Lying there in the dark, the mind, if not the body, starts buzzing with activity, and all the day's worries and problems come to the fore. Domestic problems, family problems, financial problems, work problems …

'How come I got such a fat electricity bill?'

'My bank balance is falling steadily. What can I do about it?'

'My granddaughter is twenty-eight and doesn't want to get married.'

'My new book is taking too long to be completed.'

'I'm losing hair. I'll soon be bald!'

And so on …

I switch on the bed-light and look at my watch. It's 2 a.m. Another three hours to daybreak.

At 3 a.m. I get up, go to the sitting room, pick up a book, sit on an easy chair and start reading. The book is *Dracula* by Bram Stoker. The wrong choice? Not at all. After reading for twenty minutes I fall asleep on the chair. All the vampires in the world can't keep me from sleeping.

After many years of sleeplessness I have made this unique discovery: it is easier to sleep on a chair than in bed.

And a book in one's hand is better than a sleeping pill.

35

The Afternoon Siesta

Recommended to all over forty: One to two hours' sleep in the afternoon.

Siesta time!

It's the secret to my longevity. And yours too, if you're a member of the Siesta Society.

I may not sleep well at night, but I most certainly make up for it during the day. A morning's work, a good lunch and then the joy of stretching out on a cot or a sofa or an old easy chair, reading for ten or fifteen minutes, then drifting off into a deep, dreamless sleep. Dreamless, because dreams usually come at night as interruptions, often unwelcome ones. The afternoon sleep, being a luxury rather than a necessity, is more satisfying, a stolen sweet.

DO NOT DISTURB

A placard carrying these ominous words is hung outside my front door before I lie down for my siesta. There is nothing worse than being woken up by the arrival of the postman or the courier boy or the landlady with the electricity bill or a tourist who has lost his way. Let others attend to these trifles. My siesta ruined, I am grumpy for the rest of the day, snapping at family members and quarreling with friends. But permitted a complete and satisfying siesta, I am at peace with the world, the most amiable creature on earth.

I believe the siesta was invented in Spain, from where it travelled to Mexico and then to the rest of the world, achieving a stronghold in warmer lands. For it is the heat of the day that makes one drowsy; that and a lunch in which the rice (probably pulao rice) predominates. People in cold countries haven't experienced the pleasures of the afternoon nap. They probably do all their sleeping at night, for their nights are much longer. If I was living in Finland I would probably sleep through the winter.

To be honest, I began indulging in the afternoon siesta when I was in my twenties, living in New Delhi in a small barsati, with just a small table fan at my disposal.

There was no air-conditioning in those far-off days. The fan whirring and clattering, I would stretch out before it in my underwear and sleep until sundown—or until there was a power breakdown.

Up here, in the cool of a hill station, I can enjoy my siesta at any time of the year. But the other day, some mischievous kids removed the 'DO NOT DISTURB' sign from my door, and I was awakened by a loud thumping and the arrival of my landlady with a water bill. Now I put a lock on my front door with a notice saying 'NOT AT HOME', and enter by my backdoor (which has yet to be discovered) in order to take my well-earned siesta.

We siesta-lovers have to resort to devious means in order to savour a complete afternoon's sleep.

And, by the way, it's time for lunch.

36
Dreams

Dreams can be funny too.

Last night, or rather early this morning, I dreamt I had got into the Indian cricket team (due entirely to influence, as my batting average was below 3) and I was all padded up, ready to go out and bat, when the rain came down and the match was called off. This must have saved me some embarrassment although, in one's dreams, it is possible to score a century without any difficulty.

Anyway, I woke up to find it raining heavily, the monsoon having arrived in full force, then fell asleep again and had another dream in which I had volunteered to take part in a boxing tournament. However, on my way to the venue, I lost my way (very conveniently, as I'm no boxer) and ended up on top of a hillock from which I had a great view of the bouts in progress. They were a clumsy, amateurish lot, and I could have licked them easily.

Not all dreams are so risible. Some can be disturbing, like the dream in which I am revisiting a town or city that I know quite well and I find it completely deserted—the shops, streets, schools, buildings all empty; just a few stray cats and dogs roaming about. I am alone in a deserted city. What has happened, where has everyone gone? I can only conjecture, and I am still conjecturing when I wake up.

Over the years I have kept a dream diary, describing some of my more interesting dreams. And a few have gone into the making of stories.

The dream world is, in some ways, a parallel world to our real, everyday world. I enjoy most of my dreams because in them I meet new people (as well as familiar people) and undergo unusual, often illogical experiences.

Sometimes I wonder if the dream world isn't the real one, and the real world a dream?

But this pen in my hand seems very real, and so are the words I'm putting down on this pad.

All the same, it's nice to be living in an alternative dream world where we are not in control of what happens.

And daydreaming is even better. In daydreams we are in control of everything!

37

The Longest Day

The twenty-first of June. The longest day of the year, up here in the northern hemisphere. We call it the Summer Solstice, when the earth begins to swing back on its trunnions and daylight shrinks imperceptibly once again.

Solstice means that the sun stands still. But that's an illusion. There is no standing still in any season. The earth turns, and the year turns, and sunrise and sunset change; and neither man nor his affairs stand still. This is the time of the year when the green leaf dominates the earth, when the root in the earth is the inescapable reality.

Man calls the earth his own, but his power over it is limited. He can participate, but it is Nature that rules. He has no power over the forces beneath the earth's surface; he has no power over the wind and the rain or the ocean's depth. His powers are negative. He can turn a forest into a desert, but he has yet to turn a desert into a forest.

What does summer mean to me?

It means a renewal of my interest in life, an interest that might have flagged slightly during the long cold winter months when, feeling my age, I crept beneath my razai to hide from the raging storm outside my window; the same window which, today, allows in a gentle breeze and a ladybird that has lost its way.

Summer means mangoes and lychees and wonderful fruit. It means leaves on every tree, the old and young. It means grasshoppers in the grass, crickets chirping, cicadas making music in the forest. It means a woodpecker knocking away at the bole of an old oak, doing its best to prise an insect out of its refuge. It means a barbet calling from the top of the deodar. It means beans and cucumbers growing in the fields, and the radish growing beneath the soil. The hills are alive with the song of birds and the laughter of children. This old writer closes his notebook and waters his plants.

Down in the plains the good earth is waiting for the monsoon rains. It will soon be here, quenching the thirsty soil and energizing everything that grows. Sometimes it will be too generous and man will again be in retreat.

Summer is April and May grown into June and July, with Nature working almost eighteen hours a day. Winter is a distant memory, and I must make every effort to be lazy today; like Mimi the cat, who has fallen asleep among the geraniums.

38

The Pleasures of Doing Nothing

It's any time of the day.

Mimi sits on a rug, looking at me through half-closed eyes.

I am sitting on an easy chair next to her, staring into space.

It's one of my lazy days and I am enjoying it. I refuse to work today. I shall sit in the April sunshine and gaze at the purple mountains.

Mimi and I are both lazy creatures. But that doesn't mean we are idle. Idleness is aimlessness and nonproductive; it signifies an empty head. Laziness is different. It is a quality possessed by an intelligent person (or cat) who just wants to sit back a little and watch the world go by.

Mimi is up all night, terrorizing the rodent population. We are running short of mice for her to play with. I can be up at any time of the day or night in order to finish an article or story. And then, for a day or two, I will do nothing.

There's an old proverb, 'Lazy people take the most pains'. Some people are a little puzzled by it. Being lazy myself, I know what it means. It means that when a lazy person stops being lazy, he or she is more active than most! Does that make sense? If it doesn't, it means you don't have the gift of being lazy.

By being lazy I don't mean getting up later or failing to complete one's assignments. On the contrary, I go to great pains to finish and deliver a book to my publishers on time. But when it's done I'm a free man—free to do practically nothing, just sit in the sun and count the cat's whiskers.

Yes, a lazy person is self-indulgent. We break all the rules of etiquette—receive visitors in our pyjamas, refuse to throttle ourselves with neckties, stay away from boring public functions and refuse to answer the telephone when taking a siesta.

Ah, the siesta! A Spanish gift to the world. That afternoon siesta refreshes the body and soul. If you can sleep in the afternoon it means that life is sweet, harmonious, enjoyable, *lazy*.

An angry man cannot sleep. A troubled man lies awake at night, thinking, worrying.

The lazy man needs no sedative. He *is* the sedative.

39

Favourite Trees

Most of us have a favourite tree, and it's often the one that we knew in our childhood—a tree that was easy to climb, or one that provided us with fruit, like the mango or the guava or the lychee. The one I remember best is the old jackfruit tree that grew right next to Granny's side veranda, providing us shade in the summer. It gave us jackfruits too, the flesh and the seeds making a good curry as well as a tasty pickle. It was also easy to climb, and I made friends with a pair of squirrels and a cheeky mynah.

Banyan trees fascinated me. Those aerial roots spreading outwards and taking root again created intricate passages through which a small boy could wander. Banyan trees need lots of space so that they can grow and spread without hindrance. There's a wonderful old banyan in the Kolkata Botanical Gardens, which could cover a tennis court. Unfortunately, in many of our towns and cities, roadside banyans are pruned and cut to such an extent that, without the support of their aerial roots, they topple over. But in some of our cantonment areas, where there are still open spaces, you will still find magnificent spreading banyan trees.

The peepul tree is related to the banyan. Its slender-waisted butterfly leaves twirl in the slightest breeze. It is a sacred tree and seldom felled. But it can look after itself. It will come up wherever its seed falls, and you will often see it growing from the roof of an abandoned building or in the crack of an old wall. Ghosts and mischievous spirits called prets inhabit its branches and occasionally trouble unwary passers-by. You must never yawn beneath a peepul tree. If you do, a pret might just jump down your throat and ruin your digestion!

I have a soft spot for the jamun tree, partly because I like jamuns, the acidic purple fruit it produces during the monsoon. When I lived in New Delhi many years ago, I would visit India Gate on the spacious approach to Rashtrapati Bhavan. Many jamun trees grew here, and you could buy handfuls of the fruit from the boys who collected them. My friend Sushila and I would end up kissing each other with purple lips. Sushila, a sweet girl who shared many sweet-and-sour jamuns with me.

These are all trees of a certain individuality who will grow where you plant them or where *they* decide to take root. They are trees familiar to the common man, growing in parks and gardens, or in groves like the mango, or on the roadside like the neem or the gulmohar or the beautiful jacaranda. They are not forest trees like the sal or the sheesham or the silk cotton.

Forest trees like the sal prefer the company of their own kind. They will flourish where there are other sal trees. Plant a sal tree on its own, far from its brethren, and it will wither away.

Our forests are under constant pressure from the expansion of townships and the endless building of housing estates, the industrial areas and the timber mafia. The forests diminish, and with them the birds, animals and small creatures that inhabit them.

The greenery departs and the earth turns to clay.

40
Trees Higher Up

I have described some of my favourite trees growing in the plains, and you, dear reader, will be familiar with most of them.

The flora of our mountain ranges is quite different. On the lower slopes of the Himalayas you have oak and pine forests. From 2,000 metres and up you have the deodar and other conifers. The deodar lives 200 to 300 years, a noble handsome tree, rightly called the tree of god (dev-dar).

At this height (which is the height of most of our northern hill stations), my own favourite is the horse chestnut, which changes with the seasons. You will find it growing on its own or among other trees, and it will rival, even outdo the best of them in bud, leaf, flower and fruit.

Bare in the winter, the elegant horse chestnut comes into new leaf in March, and by the end of April, its soft pink flowers hang like candelabras from a roof of tender green. The leaves darken, multiply and during the rains the chestnuts start forming. By September the chestnuts are ripe, enclosed in their rough covers. The covers split, the chestnuts fall, smooth and brown and round. The monkeys love to play with them. So do small children. Unlike the water chestnuts, horse chestnuts are not edible, although horses will eat them—hence the name!

The tree exists mainly for its beauty. And because its commercial value is limited, it seldom falls to the axe.

It is easy to grow. All you have to do is plant an undamaged chestnut in soft earth, giving it about 12 centimetres of depth, and in the spring a young chestnut tree will pop up. Over the years I have been a godfather of sorts to many horse chestnuts, planting them on hillsides or in the gardens of friends.

Horse chestnuts that I planted some thirty years ago are now fully grown, blessing me with blossoms. And they will grow into huge shady trees, given space and time.

Last autumn I decided to do some writing beneath a nearby horse chestnut tree. I stretched out on the grass beneath the tree, its leaves now golden and pink in their autumnal hues, and began composing a poem, but I'd only written a couple of lines when a large chestnut fell on my head and forced me to move. But it wasn't the tree sending me away. It was a mischievous monkey. As more chestnuts fell around me, I decided that I would do better writing at home.

41

Little Flowers

I have written a lot about gardeners and gardens, geraniums and gardenias, but it is the little flowers, especially those growing in the wild, that give me pleasure and delight whenever I come across them.

We know what we have in the garden. We have planted everything ourselves. But what grows on the hillside, in the forest, even on wasteland, has come up on its own, untouched by human hand, often blooming unseen, known only to the wind and the sun and the rain.

I was fortunate to grow up in the presence of flowers and gardens—the palace gardens in Jamnagar, Granny's garden in Dehradun, the headmaster's garden at my Shimla school—and I still have vivid memories of masses of cosmos outside our little bungalow in Jamnagar, rows of sweet peas trained to perfection by Dhuki, and the fragrant wisteria covering the walls of the headmaster's house.

But I did not come to know wildflowers, or appreciate them, until I came to live in the hills over fifty years ago. I had rented a little cottage called Maplewood, on the outskirts of the hill station. There was a small oak forest below the cottage, but beyond it miles and miles of open hillsides, beckoning me towards them. I would neglect my pen and typewriter and take off down a little path used only by milkmen and village ladies grazing their cows, and explore the slopes and grasslands of the surrounding hills.

I would go for long rambles, exploring the hillside, a mountain stream, hilltops and meadows, and I would often come across flowers that I hadn't seen before—clumps of wild primrose, traveller's joy, balsam commelina, periwinkle, buttercups ...

Buttercups! Tiny buttercups, growing on a grassy slope. I doubt if anyone noticed them, except for the sheep grazing on the hillside. And in shady, cool places near perennial springs, I found sheets of yellow primroses illuminating rocky ledges.

Summer flowers, all of them. During the cold winter months very little grows on the hillsides. Even the grass has lost its sheen, its green. But when the winter is over, the warmth of the sun brings the hillside to life again, and the first wildflower I notice is a violet, shy and timid, hiding in a crack in a rocky ledge. It is not to be touched. Wildflowers do not survive being transported to gardens. They have their own place in the sun. They shrink at the touch of a human hand. Let them enjoy their privacy.

In the spring and during the rains and in the mellow autumn months the hills were sprinkled with wildflowers, and gradually I came to know most of them, even looking up their names in books that I'd managed to obtain, such as *Flora Simlensis* and other botanical works. But of course, I saw them from the point of view of a poet rather than a botanist.

In April, the St. John's Wart flourishes, its bright yellows blooms brightening up the hillside. The tree rhododendrons would be in flower, and the milkman's son would bring me masses of them. The traveller's joy would pop up everywhere. During the rains there were ground orchids and cobra lilies; then, in September, the lovely commelina, buttercups, wild asters, wild geraniums, pericles ... Gosh! I had to discipline myself and get back to my typewriter. I couldn't live on berries and wild honey like John the Baptist. He must have had an iron constitution.

Even when winter came and the hillsides were bare, you could still find ferns, a great variety of ferns, growing near the little stream at the bottom of the hill.

Gradually, those flowers and trees and the mountain steam found their way into my stories—'The Cherry Tree', 'A Prospect of Flowers', 'Rain in the Mountains'—and instead of being distractions, they were now a part of my work as well as part of my life.

42
Grow Something!

If you are alone and with nothing to do, grow something!

Plant a seed, wait patiently for it to sprout, experiencing the delight of watching a green shoot spring up from the soil, and take care of that little sapling as though it was a child of your own (which it is, since you planted the seed). Take pride in its progress as it grows to maturity, producing foliage, flowers, fruit!

Last year I planted a pea in a small earthen pot. Just a tiny dried-up pea. I kept the pot on my bedroom's windowsill, where it received an hour or two of sunlight every morning.

Nothing happened for a fortnight. Then, one day, when I wasn't looking, up popped a couple of emeralds—two small green leaves. I was thrilled; I felt like a writer who had just finished writing a long story—something that I have also done on a few occasions!

Anyway, I watered and nurtured that pea plant over a couple of months, until it gave me several small flowers (not sweet peas, but pretty in their own way) and then peapods enclosing a number of green peas. I tasted one of them. It was sweet and succulent. I felt quite proud of myself. Perhaps I could become a farmer, grow acres and acres of peas!

Just a dream, of course. I haven't the land or the energy for farming. I'd better stick to writing. But now, when I finish writing a story (or this little vignette), I feel like Jack climbing his beanstalk. Except that I'd planted a pea and not a bean. I guess I'll never be a successful farmer.

43

The Firefly

It was warm last night, and humid, and I opened my bedroom window to let in a cool breeze. But I did not put on the light, as it would have attracted a swarm of moths. I sat there in the dark, looking at the stars. And then a star came in.

The star turned out to be a firefly.

It was years since I'd seen a firefly, and I was thrilled; because, in the past, whenever I'd seen fireflies it had been at some turning point in my life—the end of a difficult period, the beginning of something new and hopeful. I'm not superstitious, but there's something about a firefly that brings out the primitive in me. I associate them with ages long past, dark ages when night prevailed over day and these glow-worms, fireflies, jugnu, lit up the darkness.

Because of light in the darkness of the night.

Many years ago, when I lived near the forest, scores of fireflies would emerge at night, flitting across the forest glade and gliding across my half-wild garden. It was a difficult time, and somehow they were symbols of hope. Nothing much to look at in the light of day—just pulsating little worm-like insects—but in the dark they were transformed into iridescent jewels, fairy beings.

When I was very small and saw them for the first time, I really did think they were fairies. I'd been down with a fever, and my cot had been brought onto the veranda. The lights had been put out to keep the insects away. A little twinkling light travelled across the veranda, followed by several others.

'Look, Daddy!' I cried. 'Fairies!'

He told me what they really were. But I was convinced that they were fairies.

I must be a superstitious person, after all, because I still believe in fairies.

'Parees,' my dear ayah used to call them. 'They bring good luck.'

My firefly circles the room, hovers above my head, then returns to the window and disappears into the night.

44

Salute the Crow

In parts of rural England there is (or was) a superstitious custom of saluting a raven wherever you saw one. If you gave the bird a salute, you would have a lucky day. If not, you would be in for a torrid time.

We don't have ravens here, but the crow, especially the all-black jungle crow, is a close relative and I'm all for saluting one whenever I see it. It's a harmless superstition and the crow doesn't object.

There's a particular jungle crow who visits me from time to time. He sits on the ledge of my window and looks at me with his head to one side, as though he thinks

I'm a funny fellow and probably a bit of an ass. When I give him a salute he nods graciously, rather like royalty acknowledging the tribute of her subjects.

Does he bring me luck? I haven't really noticed. But why take a chance? If anyone, man or beast or inanimate object, is said to be lucky, I'll gladly give it a salute. We could all do with a bit of luck!

The world is full of superstitions and superstitious folk—like my Granny, who placed potted geraniums on the veranda steps, saying they kept snakes away. Well, they certainly brightened up the veranda! There were no snakes anyway, because a mongoose lived in the garden, and a mongoose likes killing snakes.

To return to my crow, he gets bolder by the day. Yesterday I was having my breakfast in this sunny bedroom where I write, when he hopped in, seized my boiled egg and made off with it.

No more salutes, Mr Crow.

I'll stick to an old horseshoe for good luck.

45
How to Boil an Egg

There are times in one's life—and this can happen at any age—when we are left to our own devices in the matters of food and bodily sustenance. We can't always have someone to cook for us, and eating out in restaurants and dhabas for lengthy periods isn't very healthy. There's nothing like home cooking and everyone should be able to cook a little, simply in order to improve one's chances of survival.

An egg (preferably a hen's egg) is probably the simplest and most practical of food items with which to cook a nourishing meal. You can boil an egg, or you can fry it, or poach it, or scramble it, or turn it into a delicious omelette. I have tried all these things with varying degrees of success, but for me, boiling an egg is the most difficult. I seldom get it right. Either it comes out too soft, or it's over-boiled and breaks through the shell. Frying an egg is quick and easy. But water takes about five minutes to come to the boil (especially in hill stations where the water is heavy) and I, being an impatient cook (and a hungry one), seldom give my egg enough time to firm up.

I like the idea of making a scrambled egg, but mine come out too squishy; poached eggs are dull and far too English.

An omelette—a good omelette—is a work of art, and I can never get it quite right. All my efforts could, however, result in an entertaining cookery book called *101 Failed Omelettes*. Is any publisher interested? The silence is deafening.

Of course, there are other things on which the lone ranger can survive. Tinned stuff is out, for various reasons, the main one being that I can never manage to open a tin of sardines. They have those little keys, which I usually lose or break in two.

When on my own in London for a couple of years I lived on baked beans on toast, available at any snack bar, and eventually ended up in a hospital suffering from malnutrition. That was when I took up cooking for myself. Baked beans are fine, but they should be eaten along with something else, such as an omelette, or sausages and mash, or a herring on toast.

Among things that I have learnt to cook over the years are:

1. Bread pakoras: These are simply slices of bread fried in a coating of besan (flour from channa or gram).
2. Onion soup: Basically onions, but you can add other vegetables and spices.
3. Potato mash: You can boil your potatoes and mash them up with salt and a little butter.

When I first came to live in Mussoorie, sixty years ago, I was on my own for two or three years. A kind neighbour, Mrs Sharma, gave me some cooking lessons, and I learnt to make different kinds of dal and some simple vegetable dishes. I skipped the rice because I have never cared much for it. But I tried making chapatis, and this led to Mrs Sharma remarking: 'I see you are very patriotic, Mr Bond.'

'Well, thank you,' I said, 'but what makes you say that?'

'This chapati you've made,' she said. 'It's shaped like a map of India.'

46
That Midnight Snack

Most of us, if we are not very poor, eat three meals a day—breakfast, lunch and dinner—and sometimes a snack in between. From 8 a.m. to 10 p.m. (roughly) we are constantly pushing food down our throats, into our bellies, down our intestines and then finally into a world waiting eagerly for our faecal waste. But for roughly ten hours, from the time we go to bed to the time we get up, we go hungry, we eat nothing at all!

This is most unfair.

I am one of those with a strange constitution who wakes up in the middle of the night, or at 1 or 2 a.m., with a craving for nutritional sustenance. And I don't go back to sleep unless I've satisfied my abnormal appetite. Well, I'm told it's abnormal. Personally, I feel there's nothing abnormal about feeling hungry.

I don't wish to disturb anyone in the household at that late hour, so I slip quietly out of bed and walk barefoot to the dining room without switching on too many lights. The fridge is empty. There are apples on the dining table, but I am at war with apples ever since I lost a tooth when biting into one. Besides, they go *crunch-crunch* when you eat then, and that's sure to wake someone up.

Ah, here's a bun. There's a lot you can do with a bun, but I'm not out to create anything fancy. I cut the bun in two, butter the two halves generously, spread some sweet mango chutney over the butter, and bring the two halves together again, like Laila–Majnu or Romeo–Juliet.

Voila!

I have created a mango chutney bun.

Delicious!

Happy again, I return to my bed and dream sweetly of kids bathing in mango juice, teachers sucking lollipops and tigers enjoying strawberries and cream.

(Dear reader, do excuse this little diversion into farce, but the world is a humourless and grim place these days, and it's nice to remind oneself that life can, at times, be funny.)

47
Calm and Unhurried

In Charles Dickens's novel of the French Revolution, *A Tale of Two Cities*, the hero Sydney Carton sacrifices his own life to save his double, and walks to the guillotine calm and unafraid. Others are dragged to it kicking and screaming.

Noble heroes and great men are supposed to face death without any display of emotion. In a film this takes considerable artistry. Greta Garbo, as the glamorous spy Mata Hari in the eponymous film, faced the firing squad with admirable composure, at the same time conveying to the audience her fervent desire to go on living. But then, she was a great actress.

If I were to be dragged to the scaffold I would go most unwillingly. Kicking and screaming, probably. Unwilling to part with my hold on life. For life is wonderful, even if, at times, it is a little troublesome.

To be genuinely calm and unhurried we have to be either very young or very old. My mother complained that I was always throwing tantrums, but I don't remember these. Instead, I recall the calmer passages of childhood: walking along a sandy beach, collecting seashells; sitting on a guava tree, munching guava; making paper boats and sailing them down the little canal in front of my grandmother's house. Calm and unhurried days.

We grow up, and the days become less calm and more hurried. Most of us have now to make something of our lives—find a job or a satisfying career, get married and have children, see them through school and college, get *them* married, watch them doing well or making a mess of things, retire and look forward to a calm and unhurried existence. For the greater part of our lives we have been in a hurry to do things, achieve something, and hurry and calm don't go together.

Calmness can, of course, be simulated. Look at that senior police officer dealing with a rioting crowd. He is the embodiment of calm, although mentally he may be a bundle of nerves. Or look at the dictator of a country declaring war on a neighbour. He is stone-faced, unemotional, although he may be seething behind the self-congratulatory mask of hypocrisy.

Some of us genuinely deserve a calm and unhurried retirement, and we look for means to enhance it.

An old friend, a former bureaucrat, keeps a large aquarium stocked with colourful goldfish. He spends a lot of time sitting in front of it, contemplating those silent, calm, unhurried fish. It's a form of meditation, I suppose. They are happy doing nothing, and so is he.

I tried emulating him, and went out and bought a large tank and an assortment of small fish. They made a lovely sight, gliding about in watery harmony. Then one day I found my neighbour's cat balancing on the edge of the tank, one paw in the water, attempting to scoop up a fish. I gave a shout. The cat tumbled into the tank, the tank fell off its stand, and the goldfish were scattered all over the carpet. The cat made off with one of them, and a pair of crows flew in at the open window and swallowed the remaining fish. And while I fumed, they enjoyed their unexpected repast in a calm and unhurried manner.

48
Picking a Quarrel

Two old friends were sitting on a bench, reminiscing, chatting about the 'good old days' and their shared experiences.

'You and I have never quarreled,' said one of them. 'Why don't we quarrel like other people?'

'I don't know,' said the other. 'But perhaps we could give it a try. Let's have a quarrel!' And he picked up a pretty coloured pebble and placed it between them on the bench.

'That's my stone,' he said. 'I found it and it belongs to me.'

'It's a pretty stone,' said his friend. 'I wish it were mine.'

'Well, if you like, you can have it,' said the other, and he passed the stone across to his friend.

They both burst out laughing. They had tried their best to quarrel and failed.

But sometimes it's hard to avoid a quarrel.

Once, at a literary party, a minor publisher (not mine!) kept asking me why I couldn't write a bestseller like Chetan Bhagat or J.K. Rowling, or win a Booker Prize. I wanted to empty my cocktail over his head, but I thought better of it—I could only be a loser in a quarrel involving a writer's ego—so I turned away, walked to another part of the room and joined a harmless discussion about the weather.

Avoid quarrelsome people. They vitiate the atmosphere.

49
A Game of Choices

Life is a game of choices. Not a gamble, far from it. A choice is made after some thought and consideration, it is seldom a spontaneous thing, but even so, some risk is involved.

Make the wrong choice and you can be in for a long period of disappointment and even depression. When we are children most of our choices are made for us, but once we reach adulthood, we have to start making our own choices. And the right choice can result in a lifetime of happiness and fulfilment.

Follow your mind, but listen to your heart.

Your profession, your career, your vocation; your relationships, your partnerships; your responsibilities to family, to children; your neighbourhood, your environment; all these involve the choices you make or have made.

Gentle reader, if you are reading this, you have probably made the right choice! For you are a reader of the printed word, and those who have read widely—of philosophers, saints, great men, failed men—have acquired a knowledge of human nature and are better placed to make the right choices. But even then, some of us fail to make the right choice at the right time.

We make mistakes. We can try to correct them. With a little humility we might even succeed in doing so. But most of us are too stubborn, too proud, too ziddi, to admit to our mistakes. To do or not to do, the choice is yours.

50
Laugh It Off!

Laugh it off!

That's the best way to deal with an unkind remark, undeserved criticism or even a personal insult. Your critic would like to see you lower your guard, react with anger, lose your dignity. But if you can remain courteous and good humoured, you will have taken the moral high ground and you will feel and be the better for it.

Writers can sometimes be jealous, egotistic people who try to diminish each other with sardonic or insidious remarks.

It must have been about thirty years ago when I met a cocky young journalist whose articles had been published in a few foreign papers. We were introduced to each other in the local coffee house.

'Ruskin Bond?' He tried to look as though he was making a tremendous effort to recall the name. 'Yes, of course. But I thought you were dead!'

I could see he meant this in both senses of the word—that I was dead in the physical sense and also that I was dead as a writer—forgotten, and justly so!

I was taken aback and felt a little hurt, because the barb seemed out of place at a first meeting. But I swallowed my pride and laughed it off, making a joke to the effect that I was flattered he remembered my name, at least—dead though it was in his estimation.

Later I discovered that it was in the nature of this clever young writer to make disparaging remarks about other authors. He even went to the extent of writing a mock obituary of Khushwant Singh, then our best-known author and columnist. Khushwant Singh took it in good humour. And outlived the man who wished him dead.

51

The Folly of Self-Love

Egotism, the most deadly of human vices, is symbolized by the narcissus, a scented white flower with a drooping golden crown.

In Greek mythology, the story goes that the handsome shepherd Narcissus was adored by a thousand maidens, all doomed to disappointment because he loved himself and no one else. The nymph Echo suffered the most, pining away till she was almost a skeleton. The gods felt sorry for her and changed her bones into stones, but they could not mend her broken heart.

One day Narcissus lay down to rest near a pool. The waters were still, without a ripple. Leaning over to quench his thirst, Narcissus saw his own face reflected in the water and fell in love with his own image. He suffered agonies of self-love! He fell into the pool, groping along the bottom in search of his beloved image. The nymphs prepared a funeral pyre for the drowned shepherd, but his body changed into the beautiful but drooping flower which is known as Narcissus.

Egotism, self-esteem is a self-destructive folly that has eaten away at the minds of men over the centuries, producing tyrants and dictators who can see and admire no images other than their own.

As we get older we lose our self-love, because the image in the pool or the mirror has lost its golden crown. The flower has withered, the petals fallen. But when are young we are in danger of succumbing to that reflection of ourselves in full bloom—and then tumbling into the drowning pool.

Because of self-love, when you are young, avoid mirrors. When you are old, look into them.

52
Bald and Sexy

I see a lot from my window, particularly in the early morning, when people are walking to work or just taking a stroll. From my second-floor window I get a view of their heads as they pass, and I can't help noticing that a number of men—middle-aged mostly—have bald patches on their crowns.

Bald pates seem to be on the increase. The medical term is alopecia—an ugly word that should be removed from the dictionary. Baldness is not a disease, it is a natural condition, and often accompanies intellectual qualities. Shakespeare was bald, and so was P.G. Wodehouse. Both great men.

My good father went bald at the age of thirty. At the time he was working on a tea estate in Travancore-Cochin (now Kerala), and he had to spend much of the day out in the hot sun. This necessitated wearing a sola-topee (a pith helmet) whenever he went out, and he felt that this contributed to his baldness.

Sola-topees were in fashion up to World War II, and provided some protection from stones thrown from village boys, and monkeys dropping their potty on you as you fought your way through tropical forests.

The loss or growth of hair can be due to several reasons, I suppose. Hereditary, or lack of sunlight, or the intake of certain kinds of medication. Some years ago, when I was on medication for high blood pressure, I found that the hair on my scalp was increasing. Some months later, when I had to change my medication, my hair grew scanty and started falling!

Oddly enough, bald men often have a lot of hair on their chests. They are amorous by nature. Women are attracted to them, which is probably why some actors are now going to the trouble of shaving their heads.

I have been losing hair quite rapidly in recent weeks, but I haven't noticed any special interest being taken in me by the opposite sex. But my Persian cat, Mimi, has been more affectionate than usual, so perhaps there's something to this theory.

53
A Goofy Old Man

Yes, I see a lot from my window. Right now I can see the monsoon clouds approaching, blocking out the sunlight as they pass over Pari Tibba, the hill just to the south of Landour. We have already had some rain, but the real downpour will start tonight.

Overnight there has been a change in the atmosphere. The moisture in the air has increased, the humidity seems to have brought the insect world to life—or death. There is a drowned moth in the water jug. A spider peers at me from the opposite wall. Where has she been all these months? Devouring her mates, presumably. A little beetle wanders about on the rubber plant; he has obviously lost his way. Mimi is stalking a skink, one of those tiny reptiles that appear during the rains.

Yes, rain is in the air. I can smell it. The damp earth, the rain-washed leaves of the chestnut. A pack of stray dogs rushes about, enjoying the drizzle. Yesterday they were supine, asleep in the shelter of my steps.

Today I don't see bald heads, I see umbrellas. Colourful umbrellas—pink, orange, blue, green, multi-coloured. What happened to those gloomy black umbrellas? Here's one, shielding an old lady out to buy her vegetables. As the rain stops, she shuts it and uses it as a walking stick.

There was a time when I used to walk a lot in the rain, and I was constantly losing umbrellas and buying new ones. And sometimes they were borrowed and, like books, never returned. Back in 1970, when colourful umbrellas were coming into vogue, I wrote a story, a fable really, called *The Blue Umbrella*, about Binya, a little girl I knew, and her romance and adventures with a new umbrella. The little book took off, and has been my most successful book, sales wise and otherwise too, over the years.

At noon the pedestrians scatter, for the tourists in their cars have taken over the road. It narrows down right here, with the result that a hundred cars coming up the road, en-route to the summit, confront a hundred cars coming downhill, and it can take an hour or more for the result jam to be unjammed. Fortunately the drizzle and the cool breeze help to keep tempers under control and the congestion is finally eased without too many incidents of road rage. But only last week, at the other end of town, an enraged visitor produced a kirpan and attacked a taxi driver, who is now in hospital recovering from his wounds.

Slipping between the openings in the waiting traffic is my postman, always welcome. There was a time when he brought cheques for the famished author, but now payments are transferred electronically to bank accounts. He has just one letter for me today, a little poem from a reader (called fans these days). Her name is Vidisha and she gives no address, but here's the poem, addressed to me:

> *A snowdrop*
> *Knocking on the window*
> *and an old goofy man*
> *wakes up with his typewriter*
> *cleans his spectacles*
> *and ready to drift over snow-covered mountains,*
> *to collect some pieces*
> *that drifted away*
> *along the stars,*

and he found a little piece of him
still waving
from the edges of mountains.

Thank you, Vidisha. I liked the poem and I'm still waving from mountains, but I'm not crazy about that line about 'an old goofy man'.

But then, one has to be a little goofy to survive for almost ninety years in a world that has long since gone goofy.

And I hope it will be a better world when you grow up.

54

Happiness Is History

Happy is the country which has no history.

This observation was made by a philosopher of old.

A country inherits is conflicts, prejudices, divisions, ethnic and religious differences, and it cannot change the past—a past of lost empires, failed kingdoms, invasions, migrations, the diversity of languages ... These are the inheritance of a country such as ours and it takes a very wise leadership and a reasonably wise political class to deal with the 'unhappiness' all these conflicts bring about.

There is, of course, one antidote to unhappiness, and that is prosperity. If all of us are making a good living and our families and companions are comfortable, harmony prevails. A hungry man is an angry man. And no one feels like fighting after a heavy meal.

But is there a country without a history? Greenland, perhaps. Or Baffin Island. Or some dot in the South Pacific. But those are usually protectorates and have tiny populations. Even Pitcairn Island, with its fifty-odd inhabitants, has a history of violence.

Human beings are fickle. Give them everything they want, and they will ask for more. Also, we have quarrelsome natures. We find it difficult to get on with our neighbours, let alone strangers. Somehow, hate seems more satisfying than love. You feel good after getting the better of someone you dislike.

For a change, let us try loving our enemies. If nothing else, we'll confuse them!

55

War and Peace

It's a rotten old world. But when has it been otherwise? It's a world full of hate and greed and conflict and fearful weapons of mass destruction. But when was it otherwise?

I grew up during World War II—the war to end all wars (supposedly). Hitler grabbed most of Europe, Japan grabbed most of Asia. Millions of Jews were starved to death or sent to the gas chambers. Russia suffered a merciless invasion, then threw back the Germans with equal ferocity. Japan attacked America, the war spread across the Pacific. Finally, America dropped atom bombs on Hiroshima and Nagasaki, wiping out entire populations.

I was ten years old in 1945. I saw it all from a distance, the haven of India. Came Independence and Partition, and a bloodbath in which hundreds of thousands of displaced Indians perished in communal violence. Mahatma Gandhi, the apostle of peace, was assassinated. I was thirteen, and I saw it from the haven of a school in the hills. I was so lucky.

Was it all over? Were there any more islands of peace left in the world? An island in the Pacific, perhaps? There was—until they used it to test a hydrogen bomb. You can't live there now.

The wars continue, the weapons grow deadlier. The human race produces brilliant scientists who succumb to the pressure of their leaders and create nuclear bombs and missiles far more powerful than those that were used before to annihilate our fellow humans.

We wait in suspense for these deadly devices to set into motion, as sooner or later they must be. The leaders of powerful nations do not inspire confidence. They are not ruthless Hitlers, they are fumbling Mussolinis. The helpless people of the smaller nations of Africa and Asia and South America look on in dismay.

But here I am, drinking my morning cup of tea. The sun is out, the geranium flaunts its scarlet blooms. Outside, the mountains are a lush green, for the monsoon has been generous. Dogs bark, children call to each other, a bulbul sings. All's well with the world—in one small corner, anyway. The trees do not quarrel with each other; the plants and wildflowers live in harmony; the wild creatures respect each other's space; even the insect world is balanced.

I sip my tea. What would I do without it? We are creatures of habit. We have spoilt ourselves. Take my tea away and I will be ready to go to war.

56
When All the Wars are Done

When all the wars are done, a butterfly will still be beautiful.

I wrote this line many years ago, and it is as true today as ever it was.

In the course of a battle, some trees will be broken or damaged by shells fired indiscriminately, and may even be reduced to skeletons. But when the fighting has ceased and the armed forces move on, nature will reassert itself and gradually, over a period of time, the trees will recover and will come into new leaf.

When the battle is over and the soldiers have gone, a butterfly will flit across the scarred battlefield, settle here and there on a wildflower or surviving shrub, and will finally settle on the still hand of a fallen soldier.

Nature will not be denied.

When the battle is over and the field is empty of warring men, the birds will return to the remaining trees. As the dead and wounded are carried away, the whistling thrush will sing its song and the rooks will return to their homes.

When all the wars are done, my friend, a dewdrop on a blade of grass will still reflect the universe.

57
Go with the Wind

Yes, it's *go* with the wind and not 'gone with the wind'; for when the wind has come and gone there is only silence and a void. Better to welcome the approaching wind, become one with it, and allow it to take you where it will—to great heights or through winding valleys or across great plains.

Shakespeare told us to go with the tide—'There is a tide in the affairs of men. Which, taken at the flood, leads on to fortune'—but the tide comes in and goes out at regular intervals, there is something predictable about it; whereas the wind is unpredictable, it is never still, it changes direction, it carries the clouds along, it affects our destiny ...

When I was at school I called it my 'adventure' wind. I would get excited and do something silly like slipping out of the dormitory late at night, removing the school bell from its stand, and rolling it down the hillside. No rousing bell next morning and we all slept late, having missed early morning PT. Later, I confessed to the crime and received a severe caning from the headmaster. That 'adventure wind' led me into more than one scrape. It was like a red rag to an impulsive nature.

But on the whole it has been beneficial, and helped me out of a life situation that had become intolerable.

After a year in Jersey, in the Channel Islands, living with kind but stuffy relatives, I longed to be free, to get away from that insular place and do something with my life. Late one evening I went out for one of my lonely walks along the seafront. A gale was blowing; the tide was in, and huge waves were dashing against the sea wall. I strolled along the deserted promenade, leaning against the wind, and I resolved to leave the island the very next day, and seek my fortune in London or return to India.

And I did just that—threw up a government job, packed two suitcases, said goodbye to my uncle and aunt, and took the cross-Channel steamer to Southampton. And thence to London.

It all happened within a day or two, and I never regretted the impulse that made me do it. I was still only eighteen. A good time to make your own decisions.

That 'adventure wind' has pursued me off and on throughout my life. It has led me into trouble and it has led me out of trouble. But I listen to it. It is the call of nature, and I am a pagan who must live by the laws of nature. The wind is here now, knocking at my window. I open the window in order to receive it. It is a soft wind, moisture-laden, coming from the south. I allow it to play around my room, rustling the papers on my desk. It wants me to join it outside, as it roams over the mountains. But I am no longer eighteen, I am eighty-eight and my legs won't take me very far.

Still, I can get up to the roof. And I won't fly away. There is still so much to be done.

58
Who Knows?

'Lastly, if length of Days be thy Portion, make it not thy Expectation: reckon not upon long Life: think every day the last, and live always beyond thy Account. He that so often surviveth his Expectation, lives many Lives, and will scarce complain of the shortness of his Days. Time past is gone like a shadow; make Time to come, present.'

—Sir Thomas Browne, *Christian Morals,*
Pt. III. xxx

Time passes like a shadow, and suddenly we realize that everything is behind us and we cannot expect much more out of life. Nor shall we. The present is enough. Seize the moment and make the most of it.

Now every day is a gift, or bonus. Those three score years and ten have been left behind. We made mistakes, we had failures; we did some good things, we had our triumphs. The past shaped the present; but it is behind us and unchangeable.

Be grateful for these extra days, the bonus of an extended life. Savour the moment, make it count. Soak up the sunshine. If it's cloudy, admire the cloud patterns. If it rains, take a deep breath and inhale the cool clean air, the scent of the earth.

Life is a mystery. Accept it as such and don't quarrel with it. The world we have been born into is a complex labyrinthine place, full of blind alleys and high walls. Life is not of our own choosing. Just as the dandelion scatters its seed, so does the human race, sometimes indiscriminately. Never mind, my friend. You and I have negotiated most of the perils and the pitfalls along the way, and we have come to a calm and pleasant anchorage.

Enjoy your well-earned rest. Read a little, write a little. Listen to music. Look up at the stars. See how they fill the night with their brightness. Look up at the moon. See how it fills the night with its soft lustre. An insignificant human, lost in the universe? No. You are a star too. You are a glow-worm, and you are capable of lighting up the darkness.

Open your window and look at the birds, the trees, the cats, the dogs, the monkeys, the mules ... Look at the people. No two of them are the same! That's the wonder and the mystery. No two of us are exactly alike.

Will we see our friends, our loved ones again? Will we come this way again?

Who knows?

59
These Are Our Golden Years

These are our golden years.

As we enter our seventies and eighties, we find ourselves arriving at a better appreciation of all that is worthwhile in our planet and in this world of our making.

The human race is destructive by nature, only too ready to go to war or to pollute and do away with seas, rivers, forests and our natural inheritance; but now and then along comes someone who can create something beautiful, meaningful—a great painting, a piece of music, a work of literature or philosophy, something that survives the conflicts and injustices that are the main features of human civilization, past and present. For, in spite of all the advances in science, education and technology, we are still only too ready to fly at each other's throats in the name of religion or geographical acquisitions. It has always been so, and will always be so. Human nature hasn't changed that much.

But in the darkness there is a gleam of light, and we can turn away from the ugly in order to appreciate the beautiful.

It is better to be a Rembrandt or a Van Gogh than a Genghis Khan or a Napoleon Bonaparte; better to be a Goethe than a Hitler; better to be a Tolstoy than a Stalin; better to be a Shakespeare or Kalidasa than a rapacious monarch or power-hungry dictator.

As we grow older we learn to differentiate between the creators and destroyers, and we look to the great thinkers and artists and writers to give our lives some meaning. And they *do* give us what we are looking for, because over the years we have seen both good and evil, love and hate, perfection and pollution, kindness and cruelty. As we grow old we can look back on all our faults and frailties, strengths and achievements, and come to a place of calm, the summit of a mountain, from which we can look down on the seething mass of humanity, and see both the beauty and the terror. That is our privilege.

These are our golden years. We have become connoisseurs of life. We have finally learnt to think for ourselves. We can distinguish the tremendous from the trivial.

60
'I'm on My Way!'

When I was nineteen, on my own in London, I went to the theatre to see a production of the all-Black opera, *Porgy and Bess*. A great bass baritone, William Warfield, played the role of Porgy, the disabled hero. There were many memorable songs in the show, but the one that remained with me, and which runs through my head from time to time, was called 'I'm on my way'.

It became a sort of inspiring theme song for me, and whenever I achieved something worthwhile, or tried something new or different, I'd sing out lustily: 'I'm on my way!'

So it was when my first book, a novel, was accepted by a London publisher; so it was when I packed my two suitcases and returned to India; and so it was when I threw up a good job in Delhi, took to the hills and made a living from the written word.

All the decisions involved risk. I took a risk in setting out to be a writer. I took a risk in returning to India. I took risks in throwing up not one job but several. And I took a risk in setting up my Standard (my old typewriter) on a hilltop.

But what is life without taking risks? It would be a dull affair, and we wouldn't get very far. It's the risk takers who get something out of life. There may be failures along the way—and I had my share of them—but success is always sweeter when it follows upon a series of failures. After my first book, there was a gap of ten years before I could get another published. But that didn't stop me from writing. I was a gardener with words as my only tool, and I had to keep growing something.

And now, looking back over the years, I can see that I did plant a small garden, and it has given me pleasure to grow flowers and a few weeds too. And here, in these few pages, I offer the reader some of meditations, contemplations, and cogitations. But I don't stop here. Even as I write these lines, my mind is busy with an idea for a story, a children's story, about a cat and a dog and a donkey, and I must start on it as soon as possible.

There isn't a lot of time left, but that doesn't matter. I take one day at a time, and once again I clear the decks (or rather my desk), take up a new pad and a new pen, and sing out: 'I'm on my way!'

About the Author

Ruskin Bond is one of India's most well-known writers. Born in Kasauli, Himachal Pradesh, in 1934, he grew up in Jamnagar, Dehradun and Shimla. In the course of a writing career spanning over seventy years, he has published over a hundred books, including short-story collections, poetry, novels, essays, memoirs and journals, edited anthologies and books for children. *The Room on the Roof* was his first novel, written when he was seventeen. It received the John Llewellyn Rhys Memorial Prize in 1957. He has also received many other awards, including the Sahitya Akademi award in 1992, the Padma Shri in 1999 and the Padma Bhushan in 2014. Many of his stories and novellas including *The Blue Umbrella, A Flight of Pigeons* and *Susanna's Seven Husbands* have been adapted into films.

Ruskin lives in Landour, Mussoorie. His other books with HarperCollins include *These are a Few of My Favourite Things, Koki's Song, How to Be a Writer, The Enchanted Cottage* and *How to Live Your Life*.

30 Years *of*
HarperCollins *Publishers* India

At HarperCollins, we believe in telling the best stories and finding the widest possible readership for our books in every format possible. We started publishing 30 years ago; a great deal has changed since then, but what has remained constant is the passion with which our authors write their books, the love with which readers receive them, and the sheer joy and excitement that we as publishers feel in being a part of the publishing process.

Over the years, we've had the pleasure of publishing some of the finest writing from the subcontinent and around the world, and some of the biggest bestsellers in India's publishing history. Our books and authors have won a phenomenal range of awards, and we ourselves have been named Publisher of the Year the greatest number of times. But nothing has meant more to us than the fact that millions of people have read the books we published, and somewhere, a book of ours might have made a difference.

As we step into our fourth decade, we go back to that one word – a word which has been a driving force for us all these years.

Read.

Harper Collins | 4th | HARPER PERENNIAL | HARPER BUSINESS | HARPER BLACK | हार्पर हिन्दी

HarperCollins Children's Books | HARPER DESIGN | HARPER VANTAGE | Harper Sport